YOUR PROPERTY
SUCCESS
WITH RENOVATION

There are those among us who have unusual abilities. Jane is one such person. Her ability to inspire and educate us all to take the next step in developing a portfolio to provide for the future in easily understood language is unique. This book is based on her personal investment knowledge and extensive research. There is something each and every one of us can take from it.

John Edwards — Founder and Chief Executive, Residex Pty Ltd

There are many books on real estate but few I'd recommend. This is one investors should read — sensible strategies from someone who offers knowledge, performance and integrity.

Terry Ryder — Director of <www.hotspotting.com.au>

Jane Slack-Smith is one of the true property success stories and property professionals in Australia. She combines an astute knowledge of the industry as well as of demographics to achieve the best possible outcome. Her style is easy to read and to the point; worthy in every sense of the word. And Jane is a nice person. What more do you need to buy this book!

Bernard Salt — Social commentator, author, columnist

YOUR PROPERTY
SUCCESS
WITH RENOVATION

2 PROPERTIES+
1 RENOVATION=
___
$1 MILLION *in the bank*

JANE SLACK-SMITH

Wrightbooks

First published in 2012 by Wrightbooks
an imprint of John Wiley & Sons Australia, Ltd
42 McDougall St, Milton Qld 4064

Office also in Melbourne

Typeset in 12.5/13.5 Perpetua Regular

© Jane Slack-Smith 2012

The moral rights of the author have been asserted

National Library of Australia Cataloguing-in-Publication data:

Author:	Slack-Smith, Jane.
Title:	Your Property Success with Renovation/Jane Slack-Smith.
ISBN:	9781118319277 (pbk.)
Notes:	Includes index.
Subjects:	Real estate investment.
	Finance, Personal.
Dewey Number:	332.6324

Cover image © istock photo/Amanda Rohde

Author photograph: Daniel Maran Photography

Printed in China by Printplus Limited

10 9 8 7 6 5 4 3 2 1

Disclaimer

The material in this publication is of the nature of general comment only, and does not represent professional advice. It is not intended to provide specific guidance for particular circumstances and it should not be relied on as the basis for any decision to take action or not take action on any matter which it covers. Readers should obtain professional advice where appropriate, before making any such decision. To the maximum extent permitted by law, the author and publisher disclaim all responsibility and liability to any person, arising directly or indirectly from any person taking or not taking action based on the information in this publication.

Contents

About the author   vii
Acknowledgements   ix
My story   xi
Introduction   xix

Part I: The foundations   1

1   Knowing what you want   3
2   Establishing your goals   11
3   Assessing your finances   19
4   Understanding your risk profile   27
5   Developing your property investing strategy   33
6   The Trident Strategy: minimising risk   43
7   Setting your buying criteria   55

Part II: The purchasing process   63

8   Funding your purchase   65
9   Getting your loan approved   75
10 Locating a property   87
11 Knowing your demographics   101
12 Hitting the streets   109
13 Finding a renovator's dream   115
14 Purchasing your property   131
15 The buying process   143

Part III: Renovating   149

16 Renovating for prosperity   151
17 Costing your renovation   157
18 My tips, mistakes and recommendations   165
19 Organising the renovation   177
20 Review, repair, repent and replicate   187
21 My renovation examples   197
22 Bringing it all together   213

Glossary   221
Index   227

About the author

Jane Slack-Smith started her career as a mining engineer. She was one of the first women to enter the male domain of underground coal mining in NSW, and went on to become an explosives expert. In 1997 the ABC's *Australian Story* ran an episode on Jane's experiences.

So how did Jane go from dealing with explosives to riding the roller-coaster of the property market? She made the decision to start investing her money rather than letting it sit in her bank account, and found that she had a knack for buying and renovating properties. Jane and her husband Todd now own eight investment properties, and have just completed their seventh renovation.

In 2005 Jane established her own mortgage broking company, Investors Choice Mortgages, and in 2010 she was awarded the title of 'Mortgage Broker of the Year'.

Jane is passionate about helping Australians achieve financial freedom through investment in property. She shares her experience and of low-risk property investing through education sessions and workshops. Visit Jane's website <www.yourpropertysuccessnow.com.au> for more information.

Acknowledgements

To my parents, Glennis and David Slack-Smith, thank you for giving my sister and I the gift of self-belief, access to education to achieve our goals, and for encouraging our questioning, curious minds. There can be no greater riches.

To my darling son Max, who has taught me more about myself and our world than I could have imagined. I wish for you a life full of curiosity and continuous adventures.

To my patient, generous and loving husband, Todd. He truly sees me and makes me want to be better every day — thank you.

Many people contribute each day in making me who I am and encourage me to strive to achieve all that I can. To my mentor Rolf Latham, thank you.

My story

I am no car-racing expert, but I do get the concept of the 'pole position'. If you have the right team, knowledge, experience and equipment, you can earn the right to be at the front of the pack when the race starts. If you don't start in front you have a whole lot more work to do to win the race.

So which race do we play at every day? The rat race. We go to work, earn money, come home, spend it and then we have to go to work again. Some people get to start at the front of the pack by virtue of their family's wealth and opportunity, but most of us simply have no choice but to work hard to get a glimpse of pole position.

Then how do you get to pole position so you can not only win the race, but exit the rat race? You get a head start by learning from someone who's already been there. Hi, how are you?

I didn't start in pole position, although I had the supportive, loving family every one of my friends wanted. I did not come from a position of wealth, or in fact a family with much — if any — disposable income. My parents made sacrifices to give their daughters every opportunity they could.

They also gave us amazing gifts: belief in ourselves and the education to pursue our dreams. In fact, I was the first in my family to attend university. I still remember my parents sitting up through the night putting letters into envelopes and sending them off to companies asking about scholarships and bursaries. The good news was that all that work paid off and I won a scholarship to study at the University of New South Wales.

I knew I needed an education to get ahead. I also knew that once at university I could work out what — and in fact who — I wanted to be. I just had to get there. I applied for every university course that interested me. Early on I worked out that the people on the 200 *BRW* Rich List did not have a degree in history or education, so I decided to pass on those degrees. I also knew I liked public speaking, so I applied for anything to do with public relations. I was good at maths and science so I chose to throw engineering in there as well, just in case.

After applying for several types of engineering scholarships, I received an offer for an interview from the School of Mines at the University of New South Wales. It was the day of my Year 12 graduation ball and my mind was not really 'on the ball'—rather, it was on *the* ball. I was in a pretty casual mood. The interviewers asked why I wanted to be a mining engineer. I told them, 'Well, Dad is a farmer. I come from five generations of farmers; it's about time we dug a bit deeper'. They liked my answer. I got the scholarship and an eye-opening experience for the next few years.

There were other challenges too—ones that I could not prepare for. On my first day at work at a New South Wales underground coal mine, 300 men went on strike. As legislation had just been overturned allowing women to legally work underground I became one of the test cases. The reason for the strike was that they believed it was 'unlucky' to have a woman underground. In fact, the manager's greatest concern was that the men would swear in front of me, so they had me dressed up in white paper overalls 'so they could see me coming'. Unfortunately, no-one realised that working in a wet underground coal mine 200 metres below a lake and the fact that the overalls were paper added a whole new issue to my first visit underground. Thank goodness I had a t-shirt and shorts on underneath!

For the next 12 years I did learn lots of new things: how to drive 240-tonne trucks, ventilate underground mines, be an explosives expert and blow up dirt around the world, and generally just have a really good time—and I got paid well for it. The greatest lesson though was how to *think*—specifically, how to think about risk and how to assess risks.

The mining industry offered me an incredible career and experiences. In 2000 I was awarded a Churchill Fellowship to undertake my personal project of looking at how explosives could be used for mine site rehabilitation. It enabled me to travel around the world. Not many people get the opportunity to see the beautiful forests of Vancouver by helicopter, or work in the icy north of Alaska. Actually, in the same year—as an Australian first—my sister Peta also won a Churchill Fellowship for her work on best practice management in agriculture.

This brings me back to my point: that achieving what you want is all about opportunity and belief. It is the fundamentals our parents taught my sister and myself. In fact, every parent should take the opportunity to instil this in their children. This belief can make all the difference to their future. Set your goal; recognise which resources, skills and tools you need; and believe in yourself to achieve it.

Getting to pole position

Like me, you may have made a huge investment of time in yourself and your knowledge base so that you can go out and earn a dollar, create a comfortable home, provide adequately for your family and generally enter the race everyone else is playing. The grand plans you once had of rapid career progression may not have played out as you expected. You may be on the steady corporate ladder going up one rung at a time, arguing your case at performance review time on why you deserve more than the CPI increase.

I think there are many people out there climbing the corporate ladder only to get to the top and realise the ladder was against the wrong wall.

While I did not start in pole position, I knew that investing time and money into personal education towards my career was not the end of my personal investment. I needed more to achieve my goals. I knew that not being given a start at pole position meant I needed to invest more heavily in my knowledge to get myself there.

I want to let you in on a little secret that we will explore towards the end of the book. This is probably a bit deep for now, but when you are in the race trying to get to the winner's post so you can have and be all you want, your greatest competition is yourself. You will be your greatest opponent, creating doubts and even questioning your right to want more, but you can also be your greatest cheer squad. The best thing is that *you* get to decide what role you want to play: supporter or critic.

The turning point

In 1997 I was on track to continue playing my role in the rat race. I had a great career. Everything was wonderful. I was earning a high income, helping my family financially, having some great holidays ... and my bank balance was going down consistently — which was fine because I would go to work the next day and I would be paid again.

It was on one of those holidays that I picked up a book that changed my life. In *Rich Dad, Poor Dad* Robert Kiyosaki asks, 'Do you work for your money or does your money work for you?'. At the time I thought that was a really stupid question. Of course I work for my money — I go to work, and I work so I can go home and spend it all (and just a little bit more).

And then the penny dropped. I wasn't getting ahead. I was just exchanging an hour of my time for an income. I wasn't leveraging my knowledge or my income. So ask yourself: are you spending all you earn? Are you optimising yourself to not only be all you can be professionally, but also achieving your personal goals? Do you even have personal goals, or are you just trying to get by without looking at where you're going?

I knew I didn't want to just exchange an hour of my time for dollars. I actually wanted to have money accumulating when I slept. So I looked at different ways of doing this. First of all, I looked at the stock exchange (I consider myself a bit fancy free and I had heard that mortgages tied people down). In fact, my boss kept asking me, 'When are you going to get a mortgage, because I know that you'll stay with the company once you have one because you'll be tied down'. So I looked at investing in shares. I went to the stock exchange and studied all the courses they offered. At the end of this I started doing spreadsheets and more spreadsheets, analysing companies, and when I was just about to make a purchase the company would change its board or its investing strategy and I just couldn't keep track of what was going on. At that time I started hearing that property investing didn't have to be about buying a home and that mortgages weren't such a bad thing after all, so I started doing some research.

I spent months researching. I read books. I attended as many introductory courses to property investing seminars as I could. It got to the point where I was downright confused because there were so many mixed messages. I attended the courses with two questions for the speakers: what mistakes they had made and what their successful strategies were. I found that many of them did not discuss their mistakes, but when they did, what they shared was gold. I knew I definitely did *not* want to spend years learning from my mistakes. I wanted to leapfrog ahead, straight into successful property investing — not waste time and money making mistakes. And that's what this book is all about: sharing my mistakes, knowledge and experience.

What I did learn was that everyone seemed to have different strategies. There didn't seem to be one place where I could get all the information I needed; that is, one place that would have my best interests in mind.

Then I started thinking about my skills. As an explosives engineer, I understood risk. As an explosives expert, I assessed risk every single day. I would look at the consequences of something going wrong, and I would look at the likelihood of that happening. If the consequences were really bad and I could minimise the effect of those consequences by putting some actions in place to make a risk acceptable, then we could get on with it. If we could not accept or reduce the risk, we didn't do it. Simple, really.

I started thinking I could apply the same knowledge to property investing. After all, the reason I wasn't rushing into property investing was that I was scared of the risk of getting it wrong and losing my nest egg. It was only $45 000 but it was all I had.

Then I decided to combine the knowledge of all those books, and all those seminars and courses to come up with my own low-risk strategy. I was not going to just look at risks associated with one strategy over the other, but the personal risks I faced and how to minimise those. My personal risks included: what if I lost my job, or got sick, or got it all wrong and someone would not rent my property? Risk became my main focus; I wanted to know the risks of everything and how all players in the process assessed risk. For instance, how did banks assess the risk of different property types? In essence it became all about understanding risk and understanding how I could make money while protecting myself.

Taking action

In 2001, after a year of research, I combined forces with my now husband, Todd. Armed with my low-risk investing strategies and his knowledge on locating properties, we were ready to buy our first properties in Melbourne. Although I am sharing with you 'my' strategy, I need to highlight the fact that if Todd had not been even more dedicated to successful property investing than I was, I may not have even started to look at buying properties. Truth be known, he has been the brains behind finding the properties we have purchased. Growing up in New Zealand, he had the opportunity to see a property investor increase his portfolio by leveraging one property to get to the next. Todd did the lawn mowing at this investor's properties and one day he asked, 'How are you doing this?'. The investor opened Todd's mind to the language of capital growth, rental yield and leverage.

In 2001 I bought my first property for $425 000 and used my entire savings. I handed over $25 000 to the government for stamp duty and I was left with a 5 per cent deposit. I then took out a personal loan for $50 000 and started a renovation. I applied what I had read and learned so I knew exactly how long it would take, how much it would cost and what the property would be worth at the end.

Nine months later it was valued at $700 000. So I had increased the value of the property by $275 000 in nine months with a $50 000 renovation. I knew that to achieve my goals I would have to make a significant amount of money and so I had to get it right the first time.

This fantastic result was not about being lucky or buying at the right time. It was about all the hard work and a year of planning beforehand in finding the property and renovating it to the right standard, on budget and on time. From there I developed my three-prong, low-risk property investing strategy.

Essentially we didn't just increase the property value by $275 000. In fact, Todd and I bought two properties side by side and within that nine months Todd completed a renovation on his property as well, with a greater increase in value than mine.

My simple strategy worked. I bought below the market in a sought-after area with underlying capital growth. I renovated the property up to the standard expected of the market and demographic of the area. I renovated on budget to the time frame and I created wealth. After all costs — buying costs, interest on the loan and personal loan, renovation costs, stamp duty and so on — I was ahead $175 000.

That was more than I had ever dreamed of earning in a year in my 'real' job. My next step was to go back to the bank and access the equity to do this again and again. Other than the first $45 000, I never used my own money to buy a property. I do use my own funds to pay the difference between the rent and the mortgage (plus any costs), but because of my strategy that's only a small amount (as you will see in part III). With the right renovation of the right property in the right area, your property — wherever it is located — can be positively geared. I will explain this concept further in chapter 8.

Fast forward five years from my first purchase: I decided I wanted to teach my friends and family, and then others, to do what I was doing. To be able to dedicate myself fulltime to this I needed a career that would enable me to talk to people about property and my strategy every day, and be paid for it. I founded Investors Choice Mortgages, so that I could do just that while helping investors across Australia — first-time investors and those wanting to expand their portfolios — and setting up their finance structures to enable them to achieve their goals. In 2010 I was thrilled to be voted by the readers of *Your Investment Property* magazine Australia's 'Mortgage Broker of the Year'.

Thus, property investing enabled me to leave the rat race, create my own company and be recognised for assisting other people with their property. The company has grown from me working from my spare room to having staff in Victoria, New South Wales and Queensland.

Fast forward 10 years from my first property purchase: I turned $45 000 into a multimillion dollar property portfolio by recognising the mistakes and successes of others and using my skills to create a low-risk property investing strategy and a successful company — actually, a few companies. I moved up to pole position by virtue of hard work and understanding what I wanted to achieve and the steps that would get me there.

Todd's property portfolio enabled him to stop working and exit the rat race just after his fortieth birthday. Now he follows his passion as an artist.

This book is about sharing my property success, to assist you in creating your property success. My results are not typical. Remember that fewer than 2 per cent of people who invest, will invest again. This is what I have learned — they are *my* techniques. You may like to apply these — or a variation of these — to your situation and your own goals and risk tolerance to get your results. Regardless of where you start from, as you may have noticed, there are some themes to my journey and to this book: believe in yourself, take action, invest in education, do the hard work, and understand the risks and minimise them each step of the way.

Introduction

So you want to be rich? Perhaps you're looking for a life of richness? Let's be honest: you probably want both. In fact, what you really want is not to have to turn up to work every day and struggle to make ends meet—you just want a life of choices, not a wish list that never becomes reality.

Property investing seems like an easy answer; in fact, it seems everyone is doing it. If you read all the hype, it looks easy: anyone can make a buck. But the reality is very different.

As you will find by reading this no-nonsense book on property investing and renovation, it's hard work. However, the benefits are amazing. With the information in this book, you can begin your own successful property journey. I have been a student of property investment for almost 15 years. I have read books, attended seminars, put what I learned into practice, spoken at national property investing conferences and written for many property investment magazines. I have also taught on the subject for more than five years. In short, I have invested in my investment knowledge.

So I can now share with you the three secrets of property investing distilled from all that time, effort and study:

$ It is hard work.

$ Not everyone gets it right.

$ With some diligence and application everyone can get it right.

That is what this book is about. You don't have to spend 15 years getting the knowledge and doing the research. Use me and my experience as your crash-test dummy. That way you can start making a difference to your life now.

So why do people spend so much time and effort discussing the real estate market? In essence, shelter—like food—is a fundamental requirement. From the dawn of time it has been one of our basic needs. Everyone needs somewhere to live. Not everyone can afford their own home so someone else buys them a home and rents it to them. Property investing is a direct response to a basic need.

In fact, about 65 per cent of Australians own their own home, which means 35 per cent don't. The results of an RP DATA equity report published in January 2012 revealed that approximately 43 per cent of owner-occupied Australian homes are worth more than twice their original purchase price. This means that most Australians hold most of their wealth in their home. We are a nation that values property and I find it comforting that the data shows that an overwhelming 96.3 per cent of people who own a home have a property worth more than what they bought it for.

This means that the simple 'buy and hold' property investment strategy has enabled 96.3 per cent of home owners to create wealth through property. If you look at these figures you will understand why I believe property investing is a favourable low-risk strategy for creating wealth.

The majority (65 per cent) of Australians own their own home, and more than 95 per cent of those have made money from it. However, as you will see in table 1 (on p. xxiii), only 27 per cent own more than one investment property. And with 30 per cent of Australians renting, demand remains strong for property investors. For these reasons I saw investing in property—a proven asset with future demand—as a low-risk opportunity. Neither of the basic factors—home ownership and demand for housing—is going to change in the foreseeable future. I will have the opportunity to respond to any changes that do take place because I'm in as much control of my money and future earnings as I would be with any other investment or asset class.

There's only one investment that will produce a higher result and that's an investment in yourself—specifically your health and education—which will lead you to achieving your goals.

There are two principles I have learned over the past 40 years that have held me in good stead: one from my parents and one from my university education and subsequent career as a mining engineer specialising in explosives.

First, thanks to my parents, I know I can achieve anything if I apply myself to the task and take action.

Second, thanks to mining engineering, I have learned that everything carries a risk. It's how you anticipate the risk, handle it, assess it and minimise it that will determine outcome. My husband Todd and I have a large property portfolio. Yet I have a low-risk tolerance. Everything I do is about understanding the risk and minimising it wherever possible. Property investing has enabled me to achieve my goals by leveraging a basic need (housing) and providing a service (accommodating renters) to meet that need. It was not a speculative investment; it was a low-risk opportunity.

In this book, I want to share with you the low-risk, three-prong property investing strategy that I have developed and taught to thousands of people. It's not sexy, it's not about fast money, and it's boring. At its core is low-risk investing, which I know can make people into millionaires. Throughout the book you will see references to risk, and steps for minimising risk. I will also be covering higher risk strategies—to give you all the options—but the foundations to a solid investment strategy are basically pretty boring; that is, if you do it correctly.

The Trident Strategy

I call my low-risk, three-prong property investing strategy the Trident Strategy. The three prongs represent the three ways you can make money in property using low-risk strategies. The great thing is you can use one, or—as I do and will teach you to do—use them all at once. Together they form an even more powerful way of reducing your risk in property because if you apply each of these and you get one wrong, there are still two more prongs on the fork that will help you achieve your goal.

The three parts of the Trident Strategy are:

$ Buy a property below its market value.

$ Buy in an area experiencing above-average capital growth.

$ Add value through a planned renovation, on budget and on time.

That's it—boring, but profitable. This book is essentially about renovation and how you can make money from your approach to renovating your property. However, in isolation this strategy is doomed for failure without the other two strategies, so the book is split into three parts:

$ *Part I: The foundations* looks at setting yourself up for investing and defining how and why you are investing.

$ *Part II: The purchasing process* deals with locating and funding the property that will enable you to achieve your goals.

$ *Part III: Renovating* is where you will see how to create wealth. Not only will I show you how and share my tips, but I'll also show you some of my renovations.

Should you invest in property?

I have read hundreds of books on property investing. In fact, there are 131 on my bookshelf right now. You may have read many of the same books. What I have found is that there really is not a lot of new stuff in any of them. However, each tells a story and each teaches me something new — or a new way of seeing things — or gives me a new idea on how to twist something to make it better (or — in many cases — what I should be mindful of and what not to do).

So will this book be the flash of genius that you need to make your millions? Maybe. I sure hope so. My goal is to assist as many people as I can in achieving their goals.

I have had the opportunity of being on stage with many recognised property investing experts and I've watched time and time again as the audience runs to the back of the room to buy courses worth thousands of dollars. If I had been able to afford it when I started investing I might have run to the back of the room myself. I have no doubt that these courses may help many people to achieve their goals, but it struck me that to afford the 'investment' in these courses they would have had to go into debt — or be wealthy to start with — just to get the knowledge.

That's not fair! You should not have to be wealthy to learn how to become wealthy. With that in mind I started delivering face-to-face, low-price-point courses (less than $150 for a day) where I spoke as quickly as possible and crammed in all I could. Then I realised I couldn't reach as many people as I wanted to. So I spent two years — mostly at night, while running my mortgage business during the day — developing online affordable courses that would reach a large audience.

When I was approached to write this book I realised I had the opportunity to add even more value at an even lower price point to help even more people live their life of choice. So in this book I am going to try to cover as many aspects of what I have learned as possible, to enable you to use investment in residential property and, more specifically, renovation as a tool for reaching your goals. In addition to this I hope to pass on some of the tools for not only achieving your goals but for having the confidence and belief in yourself to take action and make sure the action you take will get you the outcomes you want in your life.

Don't be surprised, therefore, if there is no earth-shattering, new, get-rich-quick scheme in this book. This is about looking at how to invest for the long term using a tried and tested technique that I have used, taught and seen others replicate. Even people with many properties have applied my teachings and optimised their property portfolios, so this can suit those of you well down the investing path. In fact, it is probably a good refresher. I know it was for me when writing the book. It made me realise that I could optimise my portfolio more in some areas, and having a chance to review my goals was enlightening. I even found a 10-year plan that I look at now and realise I achieved in less than five years. How many of you have 'become a millionaire' by realising your list of goals? I also now realise that my goal was silly and non specific. I should have — and I now do — specified *exactly* what I wanted to achieve when writing my 10-year plans.

A warning about this book: be prepared for numbers. I love facts and figures. After all, I was an engineer. I want to give you the opportunity to work things out for yourself rather than take the standard assumed figures or rules of thumb. Many of the workings will be on an associated website so that I don't waste pages of the book with facts and resources, so make sure you check out <www.yourpropertysuccessnow.com.au/ypsbookbonus> or use the QR code on the back of the book. That way, those of you who want to can either dig deep and do the numbers or just accept the end result and use that.

Can you do it?

According to the 2008–09 Australian taxation statistics, slightly more than 7 per cent of the population own an investment property. Of those 1 637 808, less than 2 per cent own more than one property. Thus, while property investing gets lots of noise, there are not many people doing it successfully and sustainably. In fact, if you look at table 1 you will see that there are fewer than 15 000 Australians who own more than six investment properties — and my husband and I are two of them!

Table 1: individuals with an interest in a rental property, 2007–08 and 2008–09 income years

	2007–08	2008–09
Property interests	No.	No.
1	1 206 627	1 195 856
2	303 359	294 158
3	91 698	88 296
4	33 552	32 011
5	13 765	13 329
6 or more	14 580	14 158
Total	1 663 581	1 637 808

Source: Australian Taxation Office, taxation statistics 2008–09

I would go as far as saying that, on average, people who have only one or two investment properties were probably not particularly strategic about their purchases. Potentially, they may even be a bit disappointed in the results they have achieved. The first investment property may have been their previous home and the second may have seemed like a good idea at the time. In fact, if they had any strategy at all they may have been lucky, let alone the three strategies I teach! Neither really 'did' anything and although they have had a dabble, it may have cost a bit of money and all in all may not have been that satisfying an experience. In fact, the properties that were supposed to liberate them from a life of corporate servitude are a bit of a pain.

This does not have to be the case. With a well thought out strategy and well executed plan, I believe that the average Australian actually only needs two investment properties to get them $1 million in their bank account within 15 years. To be honest, I know that if you apply all my research and tips you can do it sooner.

Seriously, you ask? Yes! Have a look at figure 1 to see how it can be done.

Figure 1: two properties plus one renovation equals $1 million

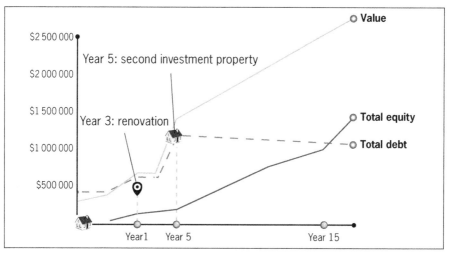

Home buyers, this is for you too!

I do want to clarify a point. The foundations, strategy and process that I cover in the book are just as relevant for those of you buying a home as those buying an investment property.

Think about it: your greatest financial investment is probably your home. What if you could use property investing strategies to understand why a suburb will outperform a neighbouring suburb? That could mean a difference of hundreds of thousands of dollars when it comes to selling to downsize or selling to get your dream home, or that decision could delay you in being able to afford your dream home. Therefore, I'm also going to consider people looking to buy their own home as property investors using property as a vehicle for achieving the lifestyle they want.

There are just a few differences. For starters, you're living in the property. Successful property investors also have their homes making money for them, but in a different way. As home owners move on average every seven years and house prices usually double every 10 years, imagine if you had investor tips and resources on hand to know where to buy houses that double every seven years or even every five years? After all, your own home may be your biggest asset, so why not maximise its value? Buy for what your family needs, but keep in mind the investing fundamentals.

Tips and bits

Occasionally throughout the book you will find 'Toolbox tips', so keep your eyes peeled for this icon:

In addition, I have much more material I want to share with you. You can access all the bonus material by scanning the QR code link below or online at <www.yourpropertysuccessnow.com.au/ypsbookbonus>.

It's time to get started on the journey to your property success. I hope you enjoy it as much as I have, and that it's every bit as profitable!

PART I

The foundations

What do you want to achieve? Until you know your answer to this question, there's no point in going forward. Before you start to learn the process of getting to where you want to be you need to work out where that is and what it looks like. You need the destination first; then comes the map to get there. There's no point taking off on a journey without a map and a destination—you're gambling on getting where you want to be, assuming that you even know where that is.

CHAPTER 1

Knowing what you want

It is unfortunate that most people don't know what they want when looking for a property — especially first-time investors. From the hundreds of thousands of properties on the market in Australia on any given day, investors choose one to purchase. Then they have to organise finance quickly, they waste time looking at many lenders, and they get so confused they end up with a less than perfect financial structure. Then they do their numbers and realise keeping the property will make things a bit tight around the house. So they read a few books on property and decide they could probably do something with the property to make the cash flow better. They ask themselves which strategy they should apply to the property. They then find out that they are restricted because they should have looked at the strategy first, before buying the property. So now they are stuck with what they have and they wonder if they will ever get to their goal.

In fact they should have it the other way around, starting with the destination, that is, their goal. They should decide on a strategy to get them to the goal, and then work out what they can afford. Knowing all this, they should assess the loan product and structure and only then should they start looking at properties.

If you follow this sequence of steps, when it actually comes to looking for a property you will have the search criteria refined so well that you can quickly assess the property.

Obviously, if you know where you're going everything else has a reference point so you will not be overwhelmed with options each step of the way. In this book we will work our way through these steps. That's why we won't even look at how to find a property until part II.

Understanding the asset

Property can be a somewhat volatile asset; perhaps not as jumpy as shares but in any given period — say, two to three years — property prices can be up or down 5 to 10 per cent (yes, down too!). Actually, the 6 per cent price drops experienced in 2011 in Perth and Brisbane were the biggest falls in the property market in more than 30 years (according to a BIS Shrapnel report to QBE, October 2011). What you read about (and I'll try not to drown you in statistics in this book, even though I love them) in the media — that is, the data they share — is often broad and based on statistical averages, means and standard deviations.

In short, individual properties can actually move up and down in price in opposite directions from the reported trends. I know when everyone was talking about market corrections and falling property prices, my well-placed properties were going up in value. They were in demand, not by chance but because of the research I had done. Over the long term, more than 10 years of property prices in most of our larger cities and towns have achieved long-term capital appreciation. You could buy in a capital city and hope that historical growth would be projected into the future and your property would go up in value. But 'hope' is not a strategy. With a well-researched and targeted investment you can do more. You should not be aiming to be average and have average returns; you want the skills to return above-average returns so you can reach your goals sooner.

It's foolish to expect an unresearched, uninformed property purchase to be a sound investment. It's possible to purchase a lemon in a lemonade suburb! As a worst-case scenario, you might be forced to sell at a time that is *not* of your choosing. Having the worst property in the area will not assist you in selling quickly. Your goal should be to have a property that people want to buy (and rent) — one that is always in demand and caters to their needs. No wonder so many people don't buy investment properties; they have probably heard of all the disasters, many of which were a result of people not prepared to do the work, the reading and the research involved in getting it right.

Regardless of 'expert' views that property prices are too high in Australia, we do have a rising income base as well as a shortage of properties and positive population growth. These things contribute to future property price growth.

The great Australian crime

The great Australian crime is happening and no-one knows it. It is the retirement myth and it is a scandal. Here is my '40 theory': we work for 40 hours a week for 40 years to retire on 40 per cent of our income. This is just at the time when we have 40 extra hours a week to do all those things we wanted to do — and you and I know they are going to cost money.

In retirement you need more than what you earn now — well, a whole lot more than the age pension (which is less than $30 000 per year for a couple). I use the word 'retirement' in the sense of reaching a stage where you have the financial freedom to do what you want when you want; in other words, a time when you can retire from your 9-to-5 job without financial worries. Obviously, working 40 years to end up with an existence rather than a lifestyle is no-one's lifelong dream.

I believe people should not trade a life of working hard for a hard life.

So once you decide that the asset class of residential property is for you, you need to determine your goals and how property will enable you to achieve them. Don't become a victim of the retirement scam.

I want to introduce you to the concept of how just a few well-placed properties can get you $1 million in your bank account (although the reality is that once you start to learn the techniques, the opportunities you discover will lead you to even greater things).

Assuming your exit strategy (we will cover exit strategies in chapter 2) is the easy one of selling your properties and putting the money in the bank, you will need to work out the value of the properties you would need to maintain your lifestyle. If the lifestyle you want to achieve will cost $100 000 per year, multiply that figure by 20 (based on a 5 per cent return) and you will find that you need to have at least $2 million of net assets earning you an income (excluding your home). So that might mean you need $5 million of property to sell with $2 million worth of loans and (after costs) you'll have to put $2 million in the bank to earn the income you want.

We will look at this later in detail and we'll also look at costs, and so on. For now, start thinking of the income you want and what you need to get you there. One thing you need to be certain of is *when* you want this income.

The time frame

Your property investing strategy will be defined by the income goal you set and when you want to achieve it; for example, an income of $50 000 per annum and a time frame of five years. Your property investing strategy is going to be a whole lot riskier than that of a person who wants that same income in 15 years' time. In this example, to achieve $50 000 per annum in five years, you may be looking at high risk and high reward development type opportunities rather than a buy and hold traditional property investing strategy. Your time frame assists you in identifying the strategy that will get you to your goal.

So, when do you want to have $1 million in the bank?

I am committed to helping Australians believe that they can have $1 million in the bank within a time frame that will actually benefit them and their existing family. I believe that by giving your existing family a better life and better opportunities, you will benefit not just your family now but also pass on your knowledge of the fundamentals of wealth creation to the generations that follow. In addition to helping the individual I believe that educating more people about how to apply low-risk property investing strategies will ensure that future property markets — and your family's financial future — are built on solid fundamentals. I believe most people buy a property based on a hunch or a tip and wonder why it never performed. This is a strategy of hope, not substance. The strategy you use to choose a property needs to have solid fundamentals so that your portfolio will sustain any economic blips. It should be based on long-term growth and growing rental yields.

The average family *can* have $1 million in the bank within 15 years. So what does an average family look like? Take a look at the example in table 1.1.

Table 1.1: statistics on the average family in Australia

Income*	Male $74 484 p.a. Female $59 634 p.a.
Credit card debt*	$3 141
Children*	2
Car repayments	$500 per month
Interest rate on mortgage	8.5%
Inflation*	3%
Median Australian property price	$444 000
Home loan amount*	$281 500
Median Australian rental return	4.35%

Source: *Australian Bureau of Statistics (ABS) November, 2010; Residex, December 2010.

I have studied these basic numbers and worked out that with the average long-term capital growth and rental yields, and based on average long-term interest rates, with just two investment properties and one renovation, the average Australian can put $1 million in the bank within 15 years. In fact, if they pay particular attention to my techniques on locating a property to invest in they can do it sooner.

You don't have to be one of the 14 580 people who — according to the Australian Taxation Office (ATO) — own more than six investment properties. You just have to have two investment properties located in the right areas bought in the next five years with one small renovation to get you to $1 million.

You can achieve a comfortable lifestyle for your family by having two well-bought investment properties that fit your strategies, time frames and goals.

This book not only assists you in setting your goals but takes you by the hand and guides you through the process of doing this for yourself. The key to this is to have solid foundations and to set yourself up correctly first, and then to find the properties with good capital growth and rental yields in the areas where you are considering buying.

The magic rule of 72

There are some considerations you need to learn that will enable you to actualise your goals. Like most things, first of all it comes down to the dollars. In the language of property investing, this is capital growth and rental yield. Rental income enables you to hold your property portfolio during your accumulation phase. Capital growth is the factor that enables you to build your portfolio and cash out to live the lifestyle you want.

There is a nifty little equation that helps you look at the relationship between capital growth and the time to get to your goals — one of those property investing rules of thumb. In this case, unlike most of the figures in property investing, you can't prove it, you just believe — just as you always know for every pair of socks that go in the washing machine one will never be seen again.

The rule of 72 enables us to calculate how long it will take for a property to double in value. This is important in that it not only relates to the passive income you need because it is directly related to the value of your property portfolio, but it also helps you work out the time fame required for achieving your goals.

Essentially, you look at the capital growth that an area is predicted to achieve; then divide this into 72 to find out how long it will take for a property in this area to double in value. For example, if you read that an area is predicted to go up in value by an average of 7 per cent per annum over the next few years, you could work out that it would take just over 10 years for properties in that area to double in value:

$$72 \div 7 = 10.28$$

So the $500 000 property that you buy today, if you find an area that is predicted to have an average of 7 per cent per annum capital growth over the coming years, will be worth $1 million in just over 10 years' time (it might grow by 2 per cent next year and then 20 per cent for four years, but the average will be 7 per cent per annum).

So it is important to link your goals to your time frame. If, for example, you want to achieve your goal of having a $5 million property portfolio in five years you will need a higher capital growth than if you allow 10 years to achieve the same goal.

These figures are based on today's dollars. Inflation also plays a part in the calculations, but for now you only need to look at the big picture. You can refine your calculations later on to allow for costs and how inflation will affect you. The main thing you need to know is that capital growth is the key to understanding how to achieve your financial goals. Just for fun, try the rule of 72 calculation with a 10 per cent per annum capital growth. Then try 12 per cent per annum. How long will it take for your property portfolio to double in value if you find an area performing better than the norm?

Capital growth and cash flow

Although capital growth is the key to achieving your goals, rental yield is important in helping you to actually keep your properties in the long term. In other words, rental income helps you pay all of your ongoing property-related costs. If you are familiar with, or have read books about, positive cash-flow properties and buying using that strategy alone, you might think that you have everything covered. However, if this is your only strategy, remember that while you can keep the properties forever as they are not costing you anything, if they are not growing in value you are going to need either a lot of properties making you, say, $50 per week, or have them for many,

many years to achieve your passive income goal. I would encourage you to look at your total portfolio realisation; that is, capital growth plus rental yield. We'll talk about this further in chapter 5.

Toolbox tip

A positive cash-flow property portfolio alone will not get you to your passive income goals. Remember that passive means you don't have to do anything. How many properties would it take at $20 a week per property to get your passive income goal? You need cash flow to help you keep and grow your portfolio, and capital growth to grow your portfolio, but then cash out and the income to live the lifestyle you want.

The rule of 72 enables you to look at the capital growth you need from your property to ensure your portfolio is valued at what you need it to be, when you need it to be, to suit your goal. This enables you to put a time frame on your goals so you can start working towards them.

The foundations of your property success are centred around understanding the property market, factors that affect it and importantly the specific requirements you need for your portfolio. In this chapter we have looked at the concept of setting a financial goal and how your goal should include a specific income amount. As we saw, for many Australian, setting a six-figure goal is possible. You can think big.

We then looked at how this can be translated into what a property portfolio should be worth to achieve that income goal and how to determine the time frame to get there. In the next chapter you are going to take these concepts and make them relevant to your specific situation.

CHAPTER 2

Establishing
your goals

Now it is time for you to look at your own situation and specify where you want to be in the future. As we discussed in the last chapter, you need to work out what your passive income goal is; that is, how much money you need to live the life you want. What is the passive income that an investment needs to generate to enable you to live a comfortable life and not just exist?

In this book, we will look at how investing in property can help you reach a goal of putting $1 million in the bank. This figure will give us an example to work through. Your goal and figures may be different, but the process works the same way.

Let's assume you want to earn $50 000 per annum of passive income. To do this, you have to work out how much money you need to have in the bank and the interest rate it needs to be earning. Let's say you are getting a healthy 5 per cent per annum interest on your money (to make the calculation simple). You would multiply $50 000 by 20 (which relates to the 5 per cent per annum earning; that is, one-twentieth is 5 per cent). So your goal is to have $1 million sitting in your bank account before taxes and fees so that you can earn $50 000 per annum.

You need to look at your long-term exit strategy. Let's assume you have a number of investment properties. (Remember that you also need to live somewhere, so we are not talking about selling your home. The properties you sell have to be income generating assets.) You sell them all, pay the real estate agency fees, the capital gains tax, the loans you're paying off, and so on, and you are left with $1 million. Obviously, the value of your assets has to be higher than $1 million to pay all the expenses.

Setting your goals

The real key to achieving your goals is to commit to them, be specific about them, be responsible to them and act on them. In fact, you could even get a friend to hold you accountable. It's fine to just write them down, but you also need a time frame for your goals and milestones or steps, each with their own time frames. The time frames have to be realistic. For example, if your goal is to go to Europe in two months' time, monthly goals may not get you there. You need weekly goals and you have to keep track of your savings and itinerary plans.

Take care of your goals, be specific, set a time frame, and identify action steps and milestones for achieving them. Then write them down, put them somewhere obvious and start visualising them. Live the life you want in your mind as if you were already there. Then it will be yours in no time.

You may already have written down your goals. If so, pull them out and review them. It's always important to review your goals and to keep them front and centre. The more you are tuned in to your goals the greater the likelihood of success.

As part of many of the training sessions and courses I run, I speak about goal setting. It is surprising how many people are willing to commit hundreds of thousands of dollars to buying property without considering why.

I cannot stress enough how important setting goals is to the outcome of your property investment aims. While it may be tempting to jump straight in and search for a property to buy, if you don't know specifically what you want, then how will you know where to start?

If your goals involve securing your financial future and you are considering a major investment, it definitely pays to take the time to sit down and work out what you want to achieve, when you want to achieve it by, and what steps you may need to take to get there.

Goal setting is especially important if you are considering investing in property with others (for example, your partner, family or friends) so that you can ensure everyone is on the same page. It's better to find out now if someone has expectations that are not in alignment with your own. I have seen many examples of joint property investment gone wrong. It always ends in tears — or worse — but in each case the damage could have been avoided or at least minimised if the parties involved had set some goals and established some ground rules upfront.

This chapter is relatively short because goal setting is something you need to spend time on by yourself. However, the chapter is at the front of the book because without clearly defined goals, your path ahead can be difficult. Obviously, there are ways of setting goals: I'm sure you've heard about having SMART goals (that is, Specific, Measurable, Attainable, Relevant and Time-bound). I am not going to write a book on this topic as there are already many books out there. As an investor you need to start at the beginning and define your goals.

Go to <www.yourpropertysuccessnow.com.au/ypsbookbonus> and download a workbook. In this you can record your goals, income requirements and asset base for achieving that income. By the end of the book you will have a summary of what you have learned, as well as your personal property investing blueprint.

Defining your goals

Many times I have asked property buyers what their 10-year financial goals are. More than 80 per cent state the goal as the number of properties they want to acquire. It strikes me that these people have no idea what their actual goal is and would have little chance of success in property investing. They don't understand that property is a vehicle for achieving wealth. As such, it isn't the number of properties they own, but the income they derive from property that should be their goal. Or — more specifically — what they want to do with that income.

In order to define your goals accurately, you need to work through the following questions:

$ What does your financial future look like if you do nothing?

$ What do you want your future life to look like?

$ How much will you need to live on?

$ What expenses will you have?

$ When do you plan to retire or release yourself to a life of having choices?

Once you have determined your goals, what you can afford, your property investing strategy and your buying criteria (which we will look at later) you are ready to start looking for a property. First, however, it is critical to have properly laid foundations—just as you do when building a house.

In the first few chapters you will notice that there is no actual mention of property and how to find the right one; that comes later, after you have defined your goals and worked out a strategy to suit your specific needs, your budget and your capabilities. The mistake most people make is that they don't start with a good foundation; they just jump straight in.

I have had the opportunity to assist thousands of Australians purchase property. In fact, I even have an award on my wall to say I have written more than $100 million in loans. I have spent more than 10 years researching successful investors and property investment techniques. I have applied this to my own investing strategies and turned an initial $45 000 into a significant property portfolio. As I mentioned in the introduction, one of the things that I discovered along this journey is that it is hard work—that's why there are fewer than 15 000 people with more than six investment properties in Australia. That's why finding someone to assist you who has done it not once but many times is difficult.

However, over the years I have applied basic foundations to property investing success and it all starts with what you are committed to achieving and by when (your goals), knowing what you need to get there (your strategy) and defining the path to get there (the process).

There's another piece in the puzzle: *mindset*. Why is it that most Australians live on less than $50 000 per annum when they retire? With all the wealth that still exists, why is it that so few Australians get to share in it? Most of us aspire to a better lifestyle. So what is going on that limits us to sharing in only a fraction of this country's wealth, and what can we do about it?

Self-sabotage is the usual culprit. Was there a part of you running around inside your mind setting booby traps to slow you down: leaving land mines, setting ambushes, blowing up your own bridges, flattening your own tyres, emptying your own bank accounts?

Do you have the mindset to achieve wealth? Of course everyone would say they want more wealth but this belies the inner voice, which may say, 'But

I don't deserve it', or 'I don't have the knowledge', or 'I was born on the wrong side of the fence so I can never be wealthy', or 'I am just too fearful to ever take the sorts of risks that wealthy people take'. I know this was one of the hurdles I had to face.

You may dream of being wealthy, but do you see yourself actually owning the house with its beautifully renovated interiors, your investment properties scattered around the country? Maybe you do. But do you actually believe you're up for the journey to get there? The inner thoughts often carry much more weight than a simple, unarticulated wish to be wealthy. How do we set our mindset, our inner thoughts? In my case I really wanted to be financially independent and away from the routine of a 9-to-5 job. I wanted to have choices about how I worked and what I did and I wanted to future proof my income for the time I no longer could or wanted to work. And I wanted investing to be a creative outlet so I could be motivated to get up every morning and — well — create. I had to release the shackle that said, 'How can I deserve more when my parents who work so much harder have so little?'. I realised by utilising not just my skills, but my resources I could assist them to have more. Their sacrifices were a choice they made to be able to give me the opportunities I received. Now it is my turn to repay the favour.

Creating and building a property portfolio is richly rewarding. Your mindset needs to be in perfect harmony with the outcome you envision and make each and every move act to support the vision. Vision is the precursor to goal setting and you will, in this book, have ample opportunity to put vision into words and actions.

Knowing your exit strategy

It is one thing to set and define your goals, but there is a whole process to follow for actually achieving those goals and we are going to jump into that soon. Although this book will cover everything on how to reach your goal income, we have to jump forward briefly to cover how you actually generate that income. It's about understanding the options available for converting your properties into the income you want. In other words, you need to know your exit strategy. Figure 2.1 (overleaf) illustrates how we are going to fast forward to the end of this process now.

Figure 2.1: the process for building a portfolio

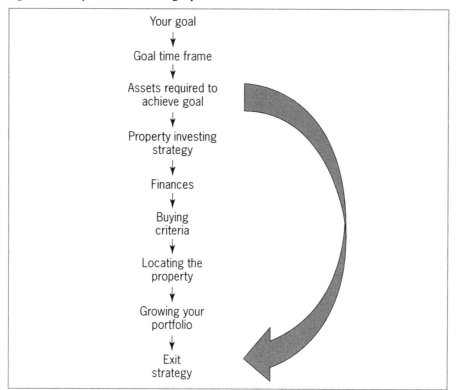

The simplest exit strategy is to sell everything once your properties are worth enough to pay off all the loans and put the funds you need to live off in the bank. There are variations to this; for instance, you could pay the loans down just enough to make the properties pay for themselves and put the leftover funds into the bank. If you had a larger portfolio, you could sell off some of your investment properties and pay off all your remaining loans, keeping those properties to generate — through their rental income — the income you desire. In this case, you may need a lot more than two or three properties. This gives you an income and you still have some properties continuing to grow in value.

If your exit strategy is to sell enough properties to pay off your entire debt you will need to consider the costs of keeping the remaining properties. Your rent has to cover not only your personal expenses but also rates, insurance, management fees, and so on.

So it is not just goals you need to think about. Your exit strategy also determines how many properties — and the characteristics of those properties — you need to reach your goals.

The important thing to remember is that the assets you are selling off must be income earning assets; that is, you cannot think of your home as an asset in this context. Net assets are calculated by adding up the value of all your shares and all your property and other investments and then subtracting the loan amounts from this. What is left over is your net assets.

If the passive income you want is $50000 per annum, then $50000 \times 20 =$ $1 million in net assets (20 being 5 per cent per annum interest return on your cash) may translate into $3 million in property with $900000 of associated loans. After you sell the properties and pay capital gains tax, real estate agency fees, and so on, you would have $1 million to put in the bank and, at 5 per cent, you would earn $50000 per annum. The $1 million stays in the bank. You never touch that amount; you just use the interest to create the lifestyle you want.

In 2007 there were 3.1 million retired Australians. Of those, 2 million were reported to be receiving full or part pensions from the government. That means two-thirds of retirees were living on less than $40000 per annum. Wouldn't it be nice to have not just an income from your superannuation but also income generated by money in the bank or your properties?

The Association of Superannuation Funds of Australia released figures in mid 2011 for the ASFA Retirement Standard that show that a couple looking to achieve a 'comfortable' retirement need $54954 a year, while couples seeking a 'modest' retirement lifestyle need $31519 a year. We all hope that our superannuation will get us at least a modest lifestyle. If not, we would be dependent on the age pension, which is currently $19522 for a single and $29434 for a couple (including pension supplements). One thing we know is that the pension does not even deliver a 'modest' lifestyle.

Courses for horses

Investing in property is a great wealth-building strategy; however, it is one that can seem out of reach of many Australians. While owning a home is part of the Australian dream, investing in property is often an afterthought. You need to have the knowledge, the determination and the resources to find out whether this is a possibility for you. Next we are going to look at what you can afford, and to understand that better we need to look at your financial circumstances.

CHAPTER 3

Assessing your finances

Now that you've defined your goals it's time to work out your finances: get to know them, understand them and work through what is possible. This involves not only establishing a personal budget, calculating what you can comfortably contribute to a property purchase and knowing where those funds will come from, but also understanding and managing your ongoing cash-flow requirements.

To be honest, in the past when I heard the term 'budget' my eyes used to glaze over. My reaction was similar to being told to 'eat your broccoli'. Now I see budgeting as a moment in time for me to work out what I can achieve. If you know you can cover your basic needs, put a bit aside for the 'nice-to haves' and still have funds left to invest, that's empowering. Many people just don't know what they can do and they assume they can't afford to invest but they have never done the numbers.

So when you think of a budget don't think of just any old boring budget but one that shows you how you can free up funds for investing (not one where you have to eat baked beans every night for dinner while you're achieving your goals). After all, if you're working at your day job, working on your property investing strategy in all the rest of your spare time and you are too broke to do anything else, it all will begin to seem too hard and you will give up on your goals. One mistake people make is that they invest and then find out they can't afford their investment, or lose sleep over it. You need to know you are in a position to invest. Don't rush in. Get to know your figures so you can work out when you will be ready, and then act.

Rather than looking at budgeting as being restrictive I prefer to take the view that it's the opportunity to never be restricted in the long term. Budgeting — or 'cash-flow management' if you don't like the word 'budget' — is going to help you avoid what 80 per cent of the population does: that is, retire on less than $50 000 per annum. Yes, that's right. Remember from chapter 2 that the government pension for a couple is just $29 434 per annum. Now that's not financial freedom by any means!

With cash-flow management it's about increasing understanding and building confidence in what can be achieved through savings and also how taking action can get you to your goals sooner.

Needs and wants: knowing the difference

Many experts suggest you allocate funds to your goals, needs and wants. Some suggest you pay yourself first; for example, by putting aside the funds to achieve your goals. This might be $100 per week of savings towards a deposit for a property. You obviously have to put funds aside for the necessities — the rent, food, and so on. Then there are the 'nice-to-haves'; for example, takeaway once a week or money for a weekend away. These last examples are discretionary spending. You should assess this area first when you look for opportunities for reducing your expenses as this is often where the biggest cuts can be made.

Reaching your financial goals means living beneath your means. It really is that simple.

You need to have savings and funds available (usually through the equity you've built up in your own home) to pay for any costs associated with a property. It is unlikely that you can achieve your goal of freedom without getting into the habit of living beneath your means. Self-discipline is vital for wealth creation. Think about it: how are you going to create funds for investment without generating a surplus based on your income and expenditure? (The difference between your income and expenses equals your potential income for investment.) The only way is by living beneath your means.

Setting up a lifestyle structure that sorts out what you really need (not what you *want*) will be a far less painful way of achieving a positive cash flow than trying to count everything you spend money on and feeling continually stressed about it. Yes, it does mean some sacrifices now, but think of your goals and the long-term benefits. That's one of the reasons you set your goals first — so you can concentrate on the end game. From personal experience and being a student of property investing for 15 years I can tell you that when you feel as though you are continually making sacrifices it can all become too difficult to bear. But it helps to fast forward five years or 10 years along your goal path and focus on where you will be and the life you will be living.

Sacrificing the Chandon for the Omni sparkling today could just get you to the Moët lifestyle you want.

You obviously want financial independence. This can be achieved, but always at a cost—only you know if you are willing to pay the price and put in the hard work. If you want to live in a world of financial freedom you'll need to give up some spending habits, and that might cause short-term pain.

This may be viewed as frugality, but frugality need not be a sentence to hardship or deprivation. Think of it this way: the definition of frugality is 'sparing, economical'. The opposite of frugal is wasteful—something you definitely cannot afford to be. Being frugal is the cornerstone of wealth creation.

There is a reason why many millionaires drive second-hand cars. They understand this concept, and in fact it probably is so ingrained in their psyche that it's a hard habit to break. When you budget you track your expenditure so that you know that $8 a day for a coffee and a muffin is actually costing you $1920 a year. You decide whether this is something you're willing to give up. If you do give up the morning-tea habit, you will most likely find that you don't miss it—just like the millionaire driving second-hand cars.

You have to be realistic about this: there's no point restricting yourself to a Spartan lifestyle—because you won't stick to it. You should certainly ensure that you don't eliminate items you really do need, such as insurance cover on your house and contents; life and sickness cover; and health insurance. But where you live and what you drive, what and where you eat, and the clothes you wear are significant targets from which to extract freedom dollars.

Discretionary items such as cigarettes, alcohol, expensive restaurants, takeaway foods, designer cosmetics and gambling expenses can be reduced, even eliminated, without affecting your lifestyle greatly. All it takes is working out what you want more: financial freedom or staying put.

Think laterally: you can still enjoy the things you want and it may not have to cost you. As you will learn at the end of the book one of the greatest gifts I was ever given was from my wonderful, thoughtful, perceptive (and very patient) husband Todd. He gave me 'Jane time'—ten days with which to do whatever I wanted, with a guilt-free guarantee.

So, we have now covered where you can save and what you should be spending your money on. Next let's look at what you have and what you owe.

Assets and liabilities

Let's digress for a few minutes while I explain how the world of banking works. When you deposit $1000 in the bank, the bank is legally permitted to lend out a multiple of that deposit. The amount of leverage it can get depends on the type of bank and its liabilities ratio. Since 1984, trading banks have been able to lend out 18.3 times the money they have on deposit, and savings banks and building societies up to 32.8 times.

Therefore, for each $1000 deposited, the bank is able to lend out more than $32000. From this example, you can see how money is created and expanded. If a bank lends your $1000 out 32.8 times at 10 per cent it would earn $3280 per annum. This interest rate could vary anywhere between 7 per cent and 10 per cent for a mortgage and up to 19 per cent for a credit card. The interest you would get in return would be between 3 per cent and 6 per cent. In essence, the bank has risked nothing and earned $3280. So you can see that the money is usually made by the bank, rather than the depositor. Wouldn't you rather be a bank?

While this is not possible for most of us, you can leverage your money so that, for example, for every $1 you contribute to a property purchase you borrow $4. Hence you contribute 20 per cent and someone else—the bank—gives you the remaining 80 per cent so you can buy a property. This is called a loan-to-value ratio (LVR) of 80 per cent

Wealth building focuses on assets. The definition that I like to use for an asset is: *something that appreciates in value and makes me money while I sleep, without having to work 40-plus hours a week.* In other words, it is something that will put money into your pocket without the need to work for it, apart from the initial effort of acquiring it, and a small amount of time to monitor it. Liabilities, of course, in the literal sense, are the opposite. Debt can be put to work in a productive fashion—for example, for buying your home or helping you buy a business — when it is applied to buying appreciating assets. It can also be debilitating and destructive when applied to depreciating assets or lifestyle. It comes down to understanding good debt and bad debt.

Good debt versus bad debt

Good debt is not a case of *not* borrowing; good debt is debt that is actively getting you to your goals. This is usually a loan that you take out to buy an investment such as shares or property. When you appreciate the difference between bad debt and good debt it is easier to make more informed choices about your spending and investment. Sometimes the fear of going into debt (any debt) underpins a fear that you 'can't afford it'.

Getting a handle on your finances

So what can you afford? You won't know what you have left over each week if you don't know what you're spending (and earning). You may be one of those people who drive around town for the cheapest petrol, but what do you then do with the $2 you saved? Does it go into a piggy bank or stay in your wallet?

Let's look at a few things you can do to get a handle on your finances.

Know your spending

Find a notebook you can carry with you and for the next week write down every cent you spend — yes, everything! This is a challenge, but it is worth it. In fact, after the first week see if you can keep it up for a month. Then you'll really start getting a picture of your financial situation and even some patterns showing why and when you are most likely to spend. Do your spending habits indicate you are an emotional spender?

Know your cash flow

If you haven't yet created a cash-flow spreadsheet, then sit down and do one. Based on the spending habits you identified above you'll have started to see where you can save. When you develop your budget it is important you include all your expenses, even the small daily ones such as lunch or coffee. Now that you have a clear picture of what you spend each week and month, look at where you could make savings if required.

Go to <www.yourpropertysuccessnow.com.au/ypsbookbonus> to download a cash-flow tracker.

Work in a buffer

You know (from your cash-flow tracker and budget) how much you have left over each month to contribute to investments and savings. But be realistic: work a cash buffer into your budget for rainy days and unexpected situations.

Decrease your spending

Write down three practical ways that you can decrease your spending. This might be as simple as taking your lunch to work. I know that's how I started saving $7 per day (more than $1680 per year). You could give up the coffee and muffin, or trade in the gym membership for your own exercise program.

Unless you are really disciplined it may help to get some friends involved in this. Friends can also help you reduce costs: instead of expensive dinners out, why not become your own masterchefs and have dinner parties, rotating the nights to different people's houses.

From an investment point of view, you could pool your resources with friends to buy property magazines each month. When I looked at my budget I found that I was spending on magazines, flowers and books. When I looked at alternatives, I saw that I could save more than $25 per week by reading magazines at libraries and even ordering latest releases through libraries at no or little cost. The $10 a week on flowers was dealt with by spending some money on pot plants. When you complete your budget tracker you will quickly see where you're spending money and you'll be able to address this. If you're like me you'll be shocked at how a few dollars here and there add up.

Reassess your credit card limits

Determine how much you really need in credit card limits. You will have taken a look at these when you prepared your budget, but did you know that a credit card limit (not balance) of $5000 will reduce your borrowing capacity by $20000 when applying for a property loan?

Look at ways to increase your income

If, having completed the tasks above, you decide you really can't afford anything at the moment — let alone a property — then let's work out how you can take action towards buying one in the future. Work out by how much you need to increase your income, then make specific and realistic plans detailing how you will go about it and give yourself a time frame in which to do it. Don't give up: now is the time to make plans and take real action to change your circumstances.

Another way of working out what you can afford to commit to investing is to first establish how much your essential expenses add up to (rates, water and all other living costs). Once you have put that money aside, deduct that amount from what you earn and allocate the difference to your savings and 'wants'. That way, what's left over can be used for investments.

In this chapter we discovered a bit about you and your finances. In part II we will go into this more deeply to see how lenders will view you and your finances. For now, though, you have a bird's eye view of your position; that is, a snapshot of where you are right now.

Next we will determine your risk profile so we can work out how to get you to your goals.

CHAPTER 4

Understanding your risk profile

Knowing the sort of future you want is a great thing, but plotting the journey and getting there will take time and hard work. First you need to draw a map. Some people want to jump straight in and risk everything to achieve what they want quickly. Others want to take a more measured approach. Take a look at figure 4.1 and think about which road you should take.

Figure 4.1: which road will you take?

Would you be prepared to stake everything and risk it all? How about risking half of your savings and current assets so you can double your asset position in 10 years? What about risking 20 per cent of your current assets to achieve the same?

Fundamentally, risk is about the *likelihood* of something happening and then the *consequences* of it happening. So if something is highly likely to occur but the result is not so bad, it could be an acceptable risk. Conversely, if it is unlikely but the consequence is a disaster, it might be unacceptable risk.

Now for the most important step: understanding how to deal with the high risks and minimising their effects. An example of a risk may be that a natural disaster will prevail—let's say a flood. The likelihood of natural flooding may be once every 30 years; the consequences devastating. So the risk minimisation plans you would have in place are to buy property outside the flood zone and to have insurance. Understanding your personal risk profile is important as it will determine what type of property investing strategy will suit you. Remember, we want you to be able to sleep at night.

All investments involve some degree of risk. Investment planning therefore is all about weighing up the level of risk you find acceptable against the potential returns. This is an entirely personal equation. There can be no one-size-fits-all approach to investment planning. And anyone who tries to tell you otherwise is peddling their own interest or simply ignorant. You must strike a comfortable balance between the level of risk you are prepared to accept and your desired level of return. The right investment strategy for you will depend on your attitude to risk and return as well as your time frame for investing. See figure 4.2 and assess your risk.

Figure 4.2: assessing risk

Probability			
Very likely	Medium 2	High 3	Extreme 5
Likely	Low 1	Medium 2	High 3
Unlikely	Low 1	Low 1	Medium 2
What is the likelihood that it would occur?	Minor	Moderate	Major

Impact

Risk tolerance

No investment is worth losing sleep over and if you are losing sleep over your investments, you haven't got the right property investment strategy in place for your risk profile.

The way each of us reacts to risk is referred to as our risk tolerance. Risk tolerance is the amount of psychological pain you're willing to suffer from your investment. If your risk tolerance is high, you may feel fairly comfortable borrowing $1 million at a loan-to-value ratio of 90 per cent to finance three or four properties. But if your risk tolerance is low, you should stick to more conservative gearing and a slower track to wealth.

You need to ask yourself some questions to determine your own risk tolerance. Do you always look for the safest options? Are you prepared to take higher risk in order to make higher returns? Do you believe cash in the bank is always the safest option?

Go to <www.yourpropertysuccessnow.com.au/ypsbookbonus> and download the quick five-minute test to determine your risk tolerance.

Dealing with uncertainty

You've bought your property, you feel like you're up to your neck in debt and suddenly things get bad—really bad! I'm not talking about personal issues such as health, job loss, relationship breakdown and the like; rather I am talking about the economic and investment environment.

Several things always happen during times of uncertainly: nervousness and fear permeate all sectors of the economy, and business and individuals tend to batten down the hatches. Another thing that tends to happen during a recession is that money becomes cheaper.

But something else happens that is much less obvious: a small sector of the community—far-sighted individuals—see the silver lining of the recessive times and take advantage of underpriced assets or opportunities that the more nervous or fearful leave alone.

So, imagine for a moment that you are one of these far-sighted Mr or Ms SmartMoney.

You always make the right decisions. During turbulent times you remain cool while others around you lose their heads. Now is one of those times. What will Mr or Ms SmartMoney do at these times?

There are only two things you can do with each dollar of take-home pay you earn: spend it or invest it. It should be natural during times of uncertainty to think twice about spending, especially on discretionary items. Vague notions of spending less, however, are not in Mr or Ms SmartMoney's language.

Smart-money people will also step into the property market during cyclical swings, especially during market panic. This opportunity arises because markets behave irrationally in difficult times. Doomsday theorists create a fertile climate for cashed-up investors to buy good quality assets at bargain prices. But you don't get to be Mr or Ms SmartMoney for nothing. It takes courage and a very long term horizon. It also takes a property investing strategy. The people losing their heads today do not have defined goals.

The economic clock

The uncertainty in global capital markets is enormous. Who knows how long it will be before earnings start growing again? Who knows how badly consumer confidence has been damaged and how long it might take to recover? Note that market bottoms occur at peaks of uncertainty.

The clock in figure 4.3 can assist you in determining the current position. In economic clock terms, when the market is doom and gloom we are probably at between 6 and 8 pm. What happens next? If you follow the clock you will see that the time will inevitably draw close to 8 pm where we can expect rising rental yields. Unlike time clocks, however, the economic clock does not tell us when the next hour will arrive.

Figure 4.3: the economic clock

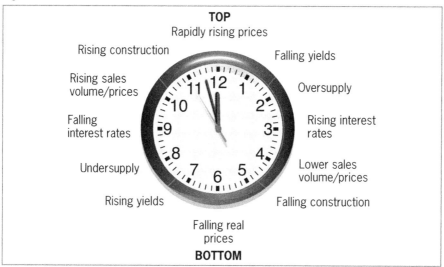

The point of even looking at the clock is to remind us that economy markets move in cycles and while there is a degree of unpredictably about the dimension or the timing of moves, a glance at the clock helps us to think rationally — not with fear or anxiety. You will hear many people say it is the time in the market, not timing the market. This is true, to some extent. New investors may decide to put off buying based on media talk about doom and gloom when in fact they are missing an opportunity. They tend to buy when the media talks about a positive market; that is, when the market is at a higher price. However, it is possible to make better returns by understanding where the market is on the economic clock.

Toolbox tip

The good news is that no matter where you live there is a market somewhere—perhaps in another state or territory—that is at the point of the clock where you can maximise your investment.

Minimising your risk

Understanding how much risk you can tolerate is important, as it will also give you a way of finalising your property investment strategy, which we will look at in chapter 5. For example, someone who has previously had all of their investments in cash (highly conservative) is probably not someone who would consider property development (highly aggressive and full of risk) as a strategy.

One way that I minimise risk is to keep my investing criteria in sync with the median house price in the market. By applying a statistical bell curve we can track what the median is and the number of properties above and below the median. More than 60 per cent of the population owns and rents close to the price range for the median. You might look at prices just a bit above or below the median to set your buying range. So if the median is $500 000 you could decide to look $50 000 above and below that median. Then you can start looking at minimising your risk by buying in this range. In fact, the ideal situation is to buy a property valued at the median but with a purchase price below that value, so that you are instantly building wealth. I suggest you look a bit above the median, as you may be able to negotiate the price down to the median or, even better, to below the median.

Toolbox tip: rules for handling difficult times

Rule 1

Don't be panicked out of long-term property investments in the face of short-term hurdles. In fact, it is invariably the time to do the opposite. Those of you with a very low risk tolerance may consider renovating rather than purchasing when things are reportedly doom and gloom. But do something!

Rule 2

Always have reserve capacity (a buffer) so that you can take advantage of rule 1.

Rule 3

If you are unsure whether your long-term investment should be in quality property or cash, look to history. The *ANZ asset returns: past, present and future* report released in October 2011 showed that residential property was the highest returning asset over the past 24 years. Even when costs and taxes were factored in, owner-occupied housing generated the highest average annual total returns (12.0 per cent), followed by investor housing (9.6 per cent) and equities (8.9 per cent).

Go to <www.yourpropertysuccessnow.com.au/ypsbookbonus> to download a copy of this report.

Now you have your goals, you know how much you can allow to help fund the day-to-day, week-to-week cash flow of a property investment and you have a feeling for your risk profile. Next you need to apply all of that to determining your property investing strategy. We look at this in chapter 5.

CHAPTER 5

Developing your property investing strategy

In the previous chapter you worked through your risk profile. Now we need to look at which property investing strategy suits you and your profile. There are so many different property investing strategies that can be employed to make money in property. In fact, with the twists and variations that can be applied these could range in the hundreds. I am always surprised when I hear about a new alternative or slant that someone has applied to an old work dog.

The first option — which most of us are familiar with — is the buy and hold strategy. That's because this is what most home owners do. In my view this should be called the 'buy and hope' strategy. They buy a property and they *hope* it is in the right area, *hope* someone will want to buy it one day, and *hope* they can sell it for more than it cost. Indeed, they *hope* they will get closer to their long-term financial goals sooner with their purchase.

Toolbox tip

Hope is not a property investing strategy. Before you start investing, ask yourself: is my property investing strategy well thought out or is it a buy and hope strategy?

Similarly, this is what many first-time property investors do. They purchase a property and hope it is in the right area, that someone will want to buy it in the future; and of course, they hope they will be able to sell it for more than it cost to buy. Indeed, they hope they will get closer to their long-term financial goals sooner with their purchase.

There is a reason why most people with investment properties never buy a second one. It's because their hopes (and dreams of financial freedom) are pinned to their investment property, which didn't quite work out as they had hoped.

Selecting your strategy

Now is the time to understand which strategy fits you and, more importantly, your risk profile.

Some of the more typical strategies that you may have heard about are:

$ renovation

$ flipping

$ development

$ off the plan

$ subdivision

$ splitting

$ wrapping

$ land banking

$ strata title development

$ commercial

$ overseas purchases

$ granny flat

$ niche (for example, student or aged accommodation).

All of these are legitimate and worthwhile investment strategies, depending on your goals and appetite for risk. Renovation, strata title development, subdivision and property development are proactive investment strategies. They can produce far greater returns than the traditional buy and hold strategy, but they are also riskier than home ownership.

In this book, we will look at two main strategies: renovation and flipping. We will not go into much detail about the other strategies because the book is about optimising your property investment through renovation.

Renovation

Renovating has become both an investment strategy and a kind of lifestyle choice for hundreds of thousands of Australians. It's even become a national pastime for television reality shows.

This investment strategy is all about buying a property and then adding value through renovation. There are low-cost renovations such as a general clean-up and replacing a few broken items, and then there are high-end renovations that involve council approval and major structural change.

In essence, this strategy is about renovating to add more dollars in value than the dollars you spend. This strategy can also deliver additional rental yield based on the renovation, which will help you pay the expenses.

Flipping

Flipping generally involves buying and selling quickly. There are a few variations, but flipping usually involves renovation. You need to be very confident of your numbers because the costs to get in (stamp duty and legal fees, for example) and the costs to get out (agents' costs and capital gains tax) can diminish any profit quickly.

So how do you make money from flipping? Most often this will be from either buying well below the actual market value; changing the usage or zoning of the property; or renovating and adding value. In all cases, within a short time frame you have a property worth more than the cost of the actual purchase (plus purchase costs).

Looking for a twist is a great way to add value to your portfolio. Remember that your property investing strategy needs to be linked to your goals and the time frame in which you want to achieve those goals. If your objective is to generate a passive income of $50 000 per annum over five years (remember that this equates to $1 million in assets, completely paid off and generating a 5 per cent income) then you may want to consider faster turnover strategies such as developing. However, be prepared—higher reward strategies come with greater risks. Figure 5.1 (overleaf) demonstrates where different strategies fit on the risk–reward curve.

Figure 5.1: risk–reward graph

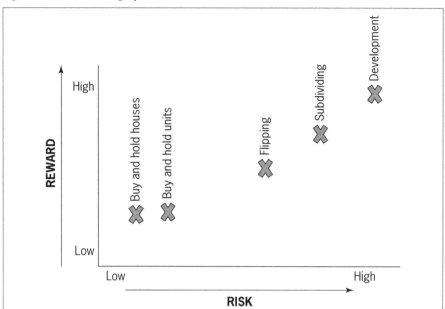

Once you understand your risk tolerance and the different property investing strategies available, you can determine your strategy and decide on the next step of refining your strategy to get you to the goal you are striving for.

Defining your strategy

Having a strategy is a vital start to property investing, but there are considerations that may affect your property investing strategy. The next step is to ask more questions about what and where you want to buy, for example:

$ Should you buy a house, or an apartment or unit?

$ Should you buy in high capital growth areas or areas with high rental yields?

Let's explore answers to these questions.

Yield versus capital growth

This remains the perennial question, especially as the tax system in Australia has a bias towards people gearing up. Our system offers capital gains tax concessions combined with negative gearing, and depreciation allowances bias individual investors towards property. Yet common sense says that the less cash you need to fund your investment the better off you are.

There seems to be a trade-off between yield and capital return: city investment prices have tended to outstrip non-urban prices in terms of capital appreciation; therefore, an inner-suburban house may have a low yield (due to the high purchase price) but demonstrate strong capital growth (historically), while a house in the outer suburbs in a regional centre might return a high rental yield but demonstrate lower capital growth.

An investment strategy that gives you a good total return on a year-on-year basis makes several early years of negative cash flow relatively insignificant when calculated over the entire investment period on an after-tax basis.

There is little doubt that wealth from property investing is created from capital gains. Even a modest 7 per cent per annum capital growth will double your total investment in less than 10 years (remember the rule of 72) and much more over 15 years, when compounding and adding additional properties to your portfolio are allowed for. Rental returns, even on a positive cash-flow basis, cannot go anywhere near matching the returns available from long-term capital growth. However, rental income is necessary for funding the costs of your property portfolio and enabling you to borrow to buy the next property. I believe you should not have to choose between yield and capital growth. By applying renovation to your property investing strategy you can have both.

Regional towns are often touted as investment 'specials' offering lower entry prices, higher yields and 'hot spot' capital gains. But there is a downside here: one-industry regional towns are vulnerable to economic shocks, which can impact savagely on property prices. Whereas a city investor only has to be concerned with interest rates and prevailing rental data (and median prices), the regional property investor also has to be concerned about the local economy.

Consider how you might minimise risks. In regional areas you don't have the multiple industries that capital cities have, which enables them to weather most economic cycles. So look at whether the regional town you are considering has multiple industries. If not, look at the next closest regional town to see whether it has multiple industries. For example, one-industry mining towns in central Queensland may be attractive due to the high rental return and capital growth. Compare these with towns such as Mackay, which has tourism, mining and ports that sustain the area, and can still reap benefits from the central Queensland mining activity.

As an investor you may feel warm and fuzzy about high regional yields, but you must look closely at the local economy. A way of getting the best of both worlds—yield and capital growth—when investing regionally is to only invest where government or industry is investing.

Traditional thinking dictates that yield and capital growth are mutually possible, as you can see in figure 5.2. However, I believe these are not mutually exclusive, as we will see later.

Figure 5.2: how growth and yield are seen traditionally

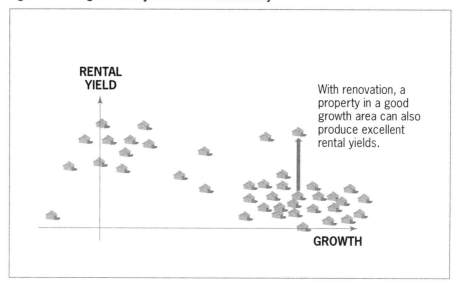

House or unit?

Is it better to buy a house or a unit? Well, that depends. A unit offers the benefit of (in general) a lower entry price into property ownership than a house would. In terms of maintenance, a house is more trouble and responsibility than a unit when you consider repairing of gutters, painting and general maintenance of the property. In the case of a unit these are the responsibility of the owners' corporation, which is of course paid by you, the owner, by way of body corporate fees.

Given affordability factors, it is hardly surprising that many people are buying units today. Increasingly, more and more people want to live within 10 to 15 kilometres of the CBD. This trend will, most likely, continue. The population of all of Australia's capital cities is increasing, and people are always keen to buy (and live) as close as possible to where they work—which is commonly the CBD. It is here that demand for units and apartments is highest. As we all know from Economics 101, when demand exceeds supply, prices go up. So if people want to live close to the action and they cannot afford to buy or rent a house, you would assume that the demand for units and apartments will increase.

Toolbox tip

Find out what the council's attitude is to new high-rise unit developments. If there is a large supply of units being built in your chosen area there may be a risk to your apartment-buying strategy as people often unit hop to the newest on the market.

You need to search in suburbs where units are going to be in demand (we will be discussing this issue often in the book). The affordability factor is important and one way to search is to literally draw a circle on a map around high-value suburbs and increase the search by extending the circle to neighbouring suburbs to yield possible investment targets. That way you may start with a more expensive suburb but gradually move towards a more affordable solution.

Those people who are just starting their property investing strategy may look to enter the market in lower value suburbs where rental returns are an important factor in building a property portfolio. However, it needs to be an area that's in demand, with good capital growth expectations. One way of reducing risk is to use your rental income to help cover your costs so you are making a minimal contribution each week from your own pocket.

Choices, choices, choices

There are so many different strategies that can lead to success in achieving your property investment goals. Each strategy has pros and cons, but choosing the one that is right for you is what's important. Determining your property investing strategy is about deciding what you want to achieve and by when, knowing what you can afford (which we covered earlier) and then fitting all of this into a proven strategy to make it all work.

The right strategy will enable you to focus your energies on finding a property that will support your goals and fit with your time frame. Just deciding on an asset type — for example, units versus houses — is not a strategy. However, if you decided to build your portfolio by purchasing only apartments and units 'off the plan', then that is a type of property investing strategy.

As we discuss strategies through the book it would be useful to focus on your goal and the time frame you are comfortable with for achieving your goal. Each strategy we discuss will generally suit a particular outcome and time frame.

Other things to consider

These are not so much strategies as things that might be useful to consider when you are defining your strategy.

Start thinking like a long-term investor and you'll start noticing opportunities as they present themselves. Opportunity comes from seeing beyond face value and also from change—for example, infrastructure changes such as a new freeway; making outer areas more accessible to a capital city; or being aware of local, state and federal legislation changes that may enable you to do more with your property or your land.

Here's an example of an 'opportunity': in 2009, a change to New South Wales State Environmental Planning legislation for multiple housing was introduced. This meant that a complying 'granny flat' of less than 60 square metres (the size of some two-bedroom units) could be added to a block of more than 450 square metres. This created an opportunity to have two properties on one title, both generating rent and hence improving rental yields.

All you need to do for now is decide on the strategy that's right for you, and continue to look for opportunities where your strategy could be applied. Remember, the reason for having a strategy is to help you achieve your goals in the time frame that you want and with the funds you have available.

Once you've decided on your strategy and started putting it into action, stick with it. After all, why tamper with something that's working?

As you articulate your property investing strategy consider how it will assist you in achieving your goals in the time frame you want. For example, a buy and hold strategy in a good capital growth area might get you to a passive income of $20 000 in 15 years' time. However, if you want to achieve this in five years' time you may be better off to consider developing. But remember: the higher the risk, the higher (and often faster) the reward.

Is renovation for you?

Maybe you have picked up this book thinking you are pretty handy around the house, so why not give renovating a go. You know: buy a 'doer upper', fix it up and then rent it out. How hard can that be?

First you need to confirm that there is renovation potential. Buying a property for $450 000 and spending $50 000 to improve it so it reflects the area's median is senseless if it is then only valued at $475 000. Second you have to ensure that the renovation you have in mind is what potential tenants (or buyers) want. Having the only five-bedroom house with a theatre room and pool in an area may be your idea of a dream house, but if the average renter in the area wants a basic three-bedroom house, you may be wasting your money. A successful renovation strategy comes down to having a plan. However, there can be many flaws to renovation plans and we'll discuss those in part III.

I have developed a three-prong property investing strategy called the Trident Strategy where renovation is the key, but the strategy is not solely dependent on renovation. In the next chapter we will look at the Trident Strategy.

CHAPTER 6

The Trident Strategy: minimising risk

You will recall that I introduced you to my property investing strategy — the Trident Strategy — in the introduction to this book. The Trident Strategy is a three-prong fork: if one prong breaks I have two other prongs to assist me in getting what I want. Remember that I am risk adverse and I believe in minimising risk where possible, so I always have a back-up plan for making money, and for getting out quickly if I have to. (However, we'll leave that for later.)

The Trident Strategy is my way of reducing risk to the absolute minimum. It's a simple strategy. As you can see in figure 6.1 (overleaf), there are three prongs on the fork. If one of the prongs breaks, there are two other prongs to back you up (see figure 6.2, overleaf).

Essentially there are three ways of making money through property investing: make money when you buy; make money in the medium term by renovating; and make money over the long term through capital growth. Hence, if one of my 'prongs' is wobbly—for example, I overcapitalise on the renovation, or I pay too much or the area does not grow as expected, I still have two strong 'prongs' that enable me to make money. The skill is in having all three working for you. That's what this book is about: teaching you to have a low-risk strategy, and also to have a backup plan.

Figure 6.1: the Trident Strategy

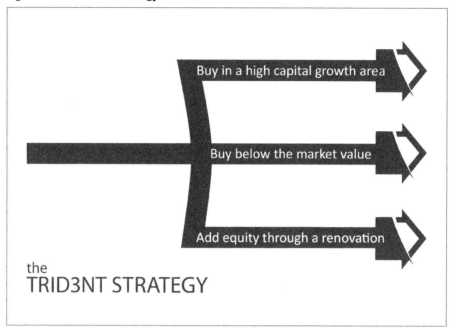

Figure 6.2: the three prongs work together to implement your strategy

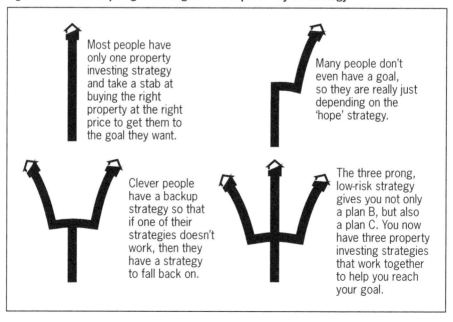

In addition to this strategy there are ways you can further reduce your risk, for example:

$ Renovate to a point just above the median so you can rent and sell faster.

$ Understand what the median property is and who the average tenant is so you know that the property you buy will be in demand, thus minimising vacancies and enabling you to sell quickly if you need to.

In this book I focus on my low-risk property investing strategy, the Trident Strategy, for property investing. You can use this strategy as it is or create your own strategy with this as a foundation.

What are the risks?

There are many risks associated with a property purchase. Consider the following, which generally apply to any property investment.

Personal risk

This is essentially the risks associated with you: not being able to afford the property, losing your job, and so on. The factors to consider are:

$ What is the risk of losing your job?

$ What is the risk of the property being vacant for long periods of time?

$ How will you cover emergencies? Do you have cash reserves you can access quickly?

Economic risk

This is largely out of your control. It is how the Australian economy is performing, how the world economy is doing and the availability of funds for buyers — and any special one-offs such as the effect of a natural disaster. Let's face it, even economists can't agree on whether interest rates will go up or down: this is hard to predict and control. You need to be aware and consider the risks. With this in mind you might want to start reading reports and listening to the market commentary to become aware of risks. These risks include tightening of banks' lending criteria (making it harder for you to get funds), high interest rates, high unemployment and higher costs of living — much of which is discussed in newspapers, on websites and by other media.

Asset risk

Essentially, lenders look at any property investment—be it a home, an investment property or a commercial property—through risk filters. They ask the hard questions that you should be asking; for example, 'If this person defaults on the loan how hard will it be to sell this property?'. Each type of property or security (as lenders consider it) has different types of risks. We can learn from lenders and how they consider risk so that we can apply their methods to our own investment plans.

If your mortgage broker tells you that your lender requires a higher deposit for a particular property it means they see it as a risky purchase and want you to have more skin in the game—and that should give you a heads up to reassess how risky the purchase is for you as well.

Consider the following scenarios:

$ a three-bedroom house within 10 kilometres of the CBD of a capital city

$ a one-bedroom, 40-square-metre unit within 10 kilometres of the CBD of a capital city

$ a three-bedroom house within 2 kilometres of the CBD of a small regional town with only one industry (an abattoir that is closing down).

Which is the riskiest? You would have to say the third scenario, followed by the second one and then the first. Why? Because if the lender—or you for that matter—needs to sell your property quickly (for example, if you have defaulted on repayments), the likelihood of being able to do this is much higher under the first scenario than the third one.

Rental risk

What happens if no-one wants to live in the property you own? What if they won't rent it at the price you want? First you need to know what makes a rental property attractive in the area where you want to buy. So, for every 10 properties you inspect in a suburb or town, I encourage you to also inspect at least one rental property in the equivalent price range. This is so you can gauge what the market wants and what the competition looks like, and so you can hear comments from people looking at the rental properties to ascertain what the potential tenants' or buyers' needs may be. (Then you'll have to do the research to confirm this.)

The beauty of the Trident Strategy is that it enables you to optimise the capital growth versus yield graph we saw in figure 5.2 on page 38. In figure 6.3 you can see that renovation enables you not only to achieve results from capital growth but also to improve your rental yield, getting you to a position of being positively geared if not straight away at least a lot sooner than the traditional way.

Figure 6.3: how renovation affects the 'growth versus yield' graph

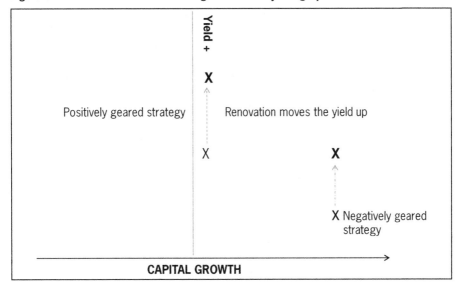

Positively geared strategy

Renovation moves the yield up

X Negatively geared strategy

CAPITAL GROWTH

Toolbox tip

Be aware of how the agent handles the 'open for inspection'. If the agent is on the phone the whole time or is an uninterested junior, then that agency is not one you should consider using to manage your property, regardless of how low their management fees are.

Not only does renovation as a strategy improve your cash flow but it also reduces your risk by making your property more attractive to tenants, and — should the unthinkable happen and you have to sell — more attractive to buyers.

There are further ways to reduce your risk, as we will discuss next. For now, however, you should be not thinking that property investing is a gamble, or that you have to be lucky to make it work. It is about looking at options and taking a low-risk approach to achieving your goals.

Minimising your risk

It's one thing to know your strategy and another to understand how to assess the risk associated with it. By now you may have a strategy in mind, but know that with every investment comes risk.

There is risk associated with you and risk associated with what you are buying, and in fact your property investing strategy also carries risk. For now, rather than consider how others (that is, the banks) will assess your risk, start thinking about how much risk you are prepared to accept for yourself and your family.

Fundamentally, risk is about the *likelihood* of something happening and then the *consequences* of it happening. So if something is highly likely to occur but the result is not so bad, it could be acceptable risk. Conversely, if it is unlikely but the consequence is a disaster, that might be unacceptable risk. You have to understand risk. Review the risk matrix on page 28 in figure 4.2 and see figure 6.4.

Figure 6.4: the risk equation

Likelihood + Consequence = Risk

Once you have assessed your risk, it's time to brainstorm the actions, strategies and steps for reducing the risk, and then assess the risk again. You need to ask yourself whether the risk has been reduced. Does the cost of putting the risk minimisation strategies in place outweigh the gain of the investment? For example, if the risk was that the ocean view of the unit you are considering purchasing could be blocked by a new property being developed on the vacant lot in front of it and the only way to keep the view is to buy the block in front, then in most cases the cost of this action would make the purchase not viable — even prohibitive.

As an explosives engineer I used to think about risk in this way for everything I did, so it was not such a stretch to apply the method to my property investing. However, most people will have to condition themselves to think about the likelihood of something going wrong. Ask yourself: what is the consequence and can I live with it? If not, is there something I can do to reduce the risk, or is this a walk-away situation? This can be anything from big-picture buying (for example, finding the location that fits with your criteria) in a one-industry town to not buying a one-bedroom unit in an area where most people want a two-bedroom unit.

The most important step is understanding how to deal with the high risks and minimising your exposure to such risks.

Devising an emergency exit plan

Before each property purchase — be it your home or an investment property — you need to have a definitive exit strategy. This is one form of risk minimisation. This does seem a little like overkill but it's one way that you can greatly reduce your risk, and improve your comfort level. For instance, if your strategy is to renovate, you might consider renovating to a standard just above the median value for the area so that you are able to rent the property quickly. This also gives you an emergency exit strategy. Here's how.

Consider that something bad (or good) happens and you need cash fast and have to sell the property. If your property is better than others in the market then in theory you should be able to sell it quickly, especially if you are prepared to accept the median price for the property. In other words, you should have a plan B for every decision you make in property investing. This will give you a low-risk property investing strategy.

Location, location, location

There is something you need to consider in order to minimise risk before you buy a property and that's to buy where people need to live. Essentially, this means buying where there's going to be long-term population growth, predominantly in capital cities or in growing multi-industry regional towns. I must stress the 'multi-industry' part of this risk-reduction plan. If you buy in a one-industry town and that industry closes down due to economic conditions, natural disasters or the like, you'll have an asset that no-one wants to buy or rent. This is particularly important in relation to mining towns as well as farming centres and even tourist centres. Remember: it is all about plan B and risk reduction.

Toolbox tip

Population growth has in the past driven capital growth and this has, over the past hundred years, been mainly in capital cities where property prices have consequently continued to grow. However, let me be clear on this: while we can't predict what will happen in the future what we can look to for guidance is what has happened in the past. It is often quoted that over the past 100 years properties have gone up by 7 per cent per annum (on average). That 7 per cent per annum is an average for all of Australia; the reality is that in capital cities it has been higher.

Look at table 6.1. Say you bought a property in 1980 in Sydney for $80000 because you got completely emotional and went over the top at the auction and spent almost 10 per cent more than it was worth. After the purchase you may have been worried. But look at the figures 10 years later. Or 20 years later. The secret to the Trident Strategy for low-risk property investing is that the safety net is capital growth. If you do get the renovation from hell and blow the budget, or you overpay, time will help heal all wounds *if you buy in the right place*.

You will find that, on the whole, when holding property for the long term in capital cities and large regional towns with multi-industries — and not trying to pick the market, the hotspots or doing anything fancy such as buying and selling quickly — prices do increase.

Table 6.1: capital city median prices

Year	Sydney	Melbourne	Brisbane	Adelaide	Perth	Hobart	Dawin	Canberra
1980	$73384	$44006	$42234					
1990	$175519	$135823	$110039		$85294			$119884
2000	$344512	$217870	$155833	$153047	$165142	$121793	$174785	$189385
2010	$667948	$600532	$457179	$408763	$489615	$385314	$517555	$534055
2011	$657028	$574360	$432009	$394023	$465489	$375550	$496684	$530500

Source: Residex <www.residex.com.au/indices>

Using rent to mitigate risk

Your property investing strategy is designed to build wealth and to provide an income for you later in life. Sometimes when property values lie stagnant for a number of years, we start to focus on rental yield. After all, it is total return that counts, but during periods where prices are relatively flat, you may look to improving yield returns to give you yield protection.

There are people who argue growth over rental yield. I believe you can have both and you should not have to compromise. The simple fact is you need a healthy rental yield to be able to afford to keep your property portfolio and you need capital growth to grow your portfolio and eventually sell up so that you have money to live off.

Initially, though, many properties will cost you money. Your job when finding a property and property investing strategy is to minimise this cost so you can get to a position where your properties are making you money quickly. You need to know how to calculate rental yield so you can make these assessments.

Rental yield is calculated as follows:

Rent per week: $250

Rent per annum = $250 × 52 = $13 000

Property value: $250 000

Rental yield = rent per annum ÷ property value

= $13 000 ÷ $250 000 × 100 = 5.2 per cent

Visit <www.yourpropertysuccessnow.com.au/ypsbookbonus> to see a list of handy calculations and definitions you will need.

Put simply, a combination of good growth and yield is ideal. In other words, your property goes up in value so that when you sell it as part of your exit strategy it is worth more than you bought it for, even after allowing for inflation ($1 now is worth more than $1 in the future). The higher the rental yield, the less you need to contribute week to week to pay for your property. For example, if interest rates are 7 per cent per annum and your rental yield is 5.2 per cent per annum, you are paying the difference of 1.8 per cent out of your own pocket (plus all the other holding costs such as rates and insurance).

It is, simply, good money management to have sufficient funds tucked away to cover the difference — plus any extra costs — of your property investment strategy for a few months. You also have to cover the day-to-day costs of your property — these are often called on-costs. Personally, I allow an extra 25 to 30 per cent to cover landlord's insurance, strata fees, property management fees, council rates, land tax and maintenance. So if the rent per annum is

$13 000 and I allow an extra 30 per cent, I would contribute an additional $3900 per annum ($13 000 × 0.3 = $3900). This is ultra conservative, but planning for the worst-case scenario is what a low-risk property investing strategy is about.

Understanding how this works is important. If you can minimise any extra costs you have to pay, and you have a property in a high capital growth area going up by more than 7 per cent per annum, then you have an advantage.

So how do you improve yield? Maybe you can negotiate to buy the property at a cheaper price. For example, if you bought a $250 000 property for $225 000, what would the rental yield be? Use the formula shown above to calculate the yield. (Hint: the answer is 5.8 per cent.)

Another way to improve yield is to renovate. This will add value to the property—but you must ensure that the value added is greater than what you spent on renovations—and hence improve the property value so you can ask for a higher rental amount. So, if you buy a property for $250 000 and you spend $15 000 on a cosmetic renovation such as painting, re-carpeting, redoing the kitchen and cleaning up the bathroom, then arguably the value of the property should be at least the initial value of $250 000 plus the value of the renovation, that is, $265 000.

However, let's assume that you derived extra value and the property is now worth $280 000. This would mean that for the $15 000 you spent you have created an extra $15 000 in value through your clever and strategic renovation decisions and execution. This could also affect your cash flow as the renovation would be funded by a higher mortgage and you may have slightly higher repayments, but remember that you will have a great boost in rent (more on this in part II).

The secret is that people with a renovation strategy try to do both: buy a property at below its true value and create equity by way of a renovation (which we will talk about in part III). Then throw in the fact that they have bought in an area with great capital growth (which we will talk about in part II and part III) and they have won the trifecta: a property going up in value, bought below the true value, with value added to it through renovation. Yes: this is the Trident Strategy at work.

Understanding rental yield enables you to work out what your portfolio needs to be achieving to minimise your out-of-pocket expenses. I rarely get into the argument about positive cash flow versus high growth and negative gearing investing strategies because I support both. My aim is to have my property going up in value and for the difference between my income and expenses to be minimal.

Borrowing with a buffer

For certain investing strategies, borrowing with a buffer may be the only risk-minimisation action you can put in place. Essentially, this means that if all goes wrong, make sure you have either equity or savings that you can use to cover the additional costs so you don't have to sell the property at a 'fire sale' price that's unacceptable to you.

If you're using equity from your home to buy an investment property and you need $100 000 to cover your contribution on a $400 000 property (that is, $80 000 deposit plus stamp duty and legal costs of $20 000), you may consider tapping into the equity with a buffer. So, instead of borrowing $100 000, you would borrow $120 000, giving you a $20 000 buffer, in case you lose your job, you can't rent the property, the development goes over time or budget or the renovation is delayed. Peace of mind is nice to have in a situation made stressful enough by other circumstances.

There are many ways to reduce your risk. Perhaps we have covered a few that you may not have thought of. Importantly, you just have to start considering every decision from the point of view of risk and minimising risk. Anything can become safe if you know how to control the risks, as I learned from explosives.

In the next chapter we're going to get even more specific. You're going to develop a checklist that you can use for assessing any property.

CHAPTER 7

Setting your buying criteria

You have determined your goals, when you want to achieve them, your risk profile and your property investing strategy, so do you think you're ready to rush out and buy? No. You need to further define exactly what it is you're looking for and where you're going to look for it.

You will read a lot about property hot spots and best suburbs as if there were a cheat sheet that could take you to your ideal property. Unfortunately, it's just not that easy. If it were, anyone with a bit of extra cash would become rich by investing in real estate. The reality is that most people never find that real-estate hot spot; they never find that dream property (or properties!) that doubles in value in the blink of an eye. In fact, very few property investors own more than one property. This statistic holds true regardless of your age, gender, nationality or country of residence. Although real-estate investing can be a money-making prospect, for most people it becomes an unfulfilled dream.

I suspect that most people never realise success in real-estate investing because they go into it expecting great things. Most people buy in the suburb where they live; when nothing really comes of their investment, they unload it as a waste of money. One of the biggest myths is that you are safer buying where you 'know'. Yet, when I ask people what they know about their area, rarely can they answer all of the following questions:

$ What is the median property price?

$ What does the median property look like (for example, two-bedroom with a carport, or three-bedroom without car accommodation)?

$ What is the largest age group?

$ What does a typical household look like?

$ Which streets are mainly owner occupied (as opposed to tenanted)?

$ What is the rent on the median property?

$ What is the long-term predicted capital growth?

$ What is the council's 10-year plan?

$ How do the majority of people get to work?

And the list goes on. So ask yourself—and be honest—how many of those questions can you answer about your suburb?

To truly know an area you need to know who lives there: this is the demographics of the area.

Demographics

The demographic data of an area is a snapshot. It gives you, the investor, an instant 'feel' for the type of person buying into an area. This, then, is an indicator of:

$ who lives there

$ how old the majority of people living there are

$ how many people live in each household (on average)

$ whether the majority drive or catch public transport

$ what the average rent is.

Each area has its own unique demographics. The type of housing in a particular area is related to its location and the demographic. Inner-city areas are much more likely to attract singles and as such would often have denser housing developments such as apartments, town houses and villas.

Investors invariably compare properties when making their investment decisions. It is important, therefore, to focus on the things that matter. The colour of a wall doesn't matter a great deal as it can be repainted cheaply. Similarly, the condition of the lawn doesn't matter much. For sure, the presentation of a house matters, but ultimately its value lies in its capacity for value adding by, for example, renovation, adding floor space or adding a level as well as buying in an area where demand will increase faster than available supply.

Understanding the criteria

Now that you know who lives in the area, you need to know what type of property they are living in. In this chapter we will drill down to the specifics; that is, what the property you want is going to look like. We essentially want a list of criteria that a property has to comply with for you to be able to check any future purchase against. If it does not match your criteria then it's a walk-away decision for you. This is where we take all the guesswork and emotion out of your purchase.

By now you will have considered your property investing strategy: you know what you are going to focus on and what type of property you want to buy. This applies equally to buying a home and purchasing an investment property. Knowing how to select a property to suit not just your short-term requirements but also your long-term goals is going to get you to your goals sooner, regardless of why you're buying the property.

In chapter 5 we looked at your property investing strategy. As you can imagine, every property investing strategy also has specific property criteria.

For example, let's assume your property investing strategy is to purchase property in good growth areas and then to create extra equity by building a house on the back of the block; that is, creating two rental streams on one property and improving the rental yield. However, you need to know the specifics of such a strategy. That's where the property criteria come in.

For this example, your property criteria might include the following:

$ The property must meet the local council's requirements for land size for a second dwelling (for example, 800 m^2).

$ The council in the nominated suburb has a history of processing and approving development applications quickly and with ease to ensure downtime is reduced.

$ The existing property must be ready to rent immediately to generate an income while development plans are being drawn up.

$ The budget required to renovate the existing property cannot exceed $10 000 (including a contingency figure).

Later, in chapter 10, we will go into more detail on how to determine the characteristics of a particular suburb or town. We will also cover how to determine what the typical property and household for that area looks like, so if you are going to purchase in that area you will know what kind of properties the people in that area want to live in, and what you should buy.

Using this information, you might define some of the following as your market criteria for the area you choose:

$ The property is a 10-minute drive from the local schools.

$ The property is a 10-minute drive from a large shopping centre.

$ The property is in an area that represents the catchment of a highly ranked secondary college. (Note that some streets within a suburb may not be in the catchment.)

$ The area is 'safe' — properties in the area are not covered with security screens; there is no graffiti; when you walk the streets you feel secure.

In total, there are three types of criteria to look at when determining your buying criteria. These are:

$ criteria that fit your property investing strategy

$ criteria that relate to the market

$ criteria that fit your personal strategy.

Let's have a look at each of these criteria in more detail.

Property investing strategy criteria

These are the criteria directly linked to your property investing strategy. For a renovation strategy your criteria may include the following:

$ the renovation needs to be cosmetic only, nothing structural

$ the budget required would be less than X thousand dollars

$ the property purchase price is 30 per cent below the median of the area (more about this in part III)

$ the profit is at least 15 per cent of the purchase price.

The property investing strategy criteria on your checklist have to be met before you would consider a purchase. For instance, if you found a property that met your market criteria and your personal criteria, but it had white ant damage and required significant structural works, then you would discard it as a possibility and move on.

Toolbox tip

If you are trying to estimate future rental income, use a conservative figure of 4 per cent per annum rental yield and include this in any servicing calculators you try. This means that, for example, a property worth $400 000 with a rental yield of 4 per cent would return a rental income of $16 000 per annum ($400 000 × 0.04), or $308 per week ($16 000 ÷ 52).

Market criteria

So how do you develop a checklist of the exact requirements you would like met before you will consider purchasing a property? Remember: it's important to 'buy where people want to live'. Also, note the demographics of the area so you can better understand who is buying and renting. This may be significant if, for example, the economy slows down and certain sectors of the area's workforce are vulnerable to becoming unemployed.

It's important that people want to live in the property as tenants. As an investor, this is about keeping long-term tenants to avoid re-letting fees and the expense of cleaning up a property between tenancies. For owner-occupiers it's about being clear on what you want so that emotion does not cloud your purchasing decision. This covers additional criteria you may like to consider; for example, the demographic may require you to be able to house a family who are dependent on using a car to get to work (so they may need at least two bedrooms and a garage or carport). Your demographics will help you define what the market wants.

This information can be sourced from the Australian Bureau of Statistics directly. However, most online real-estate sites have a suburb profile tab that shows you the key demographic information.

Personal criteria

These are your specific numbers. You've already examined your risk profile and how that will guide your property investing strategy. While your goals will help keep 'an eye on the prize', your personal criteria will guide you on what size portfolio you need in order to achieve your desired figure within the time frame you have defined.

The figure is a combination of the purchase price you can afford, estimated capital growth and rental yield predictions. These form your personal criteria.

Your personal criteria may include the following:

$ that the median purchase price must be $350 000

$ that the area needs to have a predicted capital growth above the average of 7 per cent

$ that the rental yield must be 5 per cent or more post building or purchase.

You may like to think about other personal criteria that are important to you when purchasing an investment property.

As you can see, there are specifics for each strategy. You just need to know what they are for your chosen strategy. Obviously, each of the points above will determine how much profit you make. You also know how to work out how long it will take for you to get to your goal. (Remember the rule of 72? For example, a property worth $350 000 will be worth double this amount in 10 years' time at 7 per cent per annum growth.)

Buying criteria for units

The buying criteria for units will depend on the strategy you have chosen. For example, if you want the opportunity to renovate, your strategy would dictate that you look at buying an older unit. Or, if you are not looking to renovate, your strategy would be focused on buying a brand new or newly renovated unit. Once you have determined your initial strategy, here are some additional buying criteria you may want to consider:

$ The unit must be in a block of no more than three storeys (avoid buildings with lifts as they tend to have a much higher strata levy).

$ The strata management fees and maintenance costs must be reasonable. So, for example, you wouldn't buy a unit in a block that has extras facilities such as a lift or a gym.

$ The unit should preferably not be on the ground floor (for security reasons).

$ If the unit is on the ground floor it must have exclusive access to an outside living space.

$ The body corporate must have a proven history of allowing renovations.

$ There must be a high proportion of owner-occupiers in the block.

$ There must be a carpark or lock-up storage.

Establishing your criteria using these headings as a guide will enable you to quickly and competently assess every property you come across. It will also enable you to determine whether the property is congruent with your chosen strategy and financial goals.

Visit <www.yourpropertysuccessnow.com.au/ypsbookbonus> for my personal buying criteria.

Now you have a checklist that you can refer to when you go shopping. So, are you ready to start looking at properties now? Actually, no. First you need to know how much you have available to spend and which loan structure will suit you. That's what we'll be discussing in part II with the fun bit — locating the property.

PART II

The purchasing process

This part of the book is all about your financial structure and how to set it up correctly in readiness for buying your investment property. Although considered 'dry' and 'boring', knowing the numbers behind your purchase is very important if you want to maximise your property investments. Many books skim over the financial aspects of investing in property. Yet, to be a successful property investor you must cover all the details, including financing, researching, buying, renovating and managing. It sounds tedious, but the success or failure of your execution can come down to missing one of these steps. We do finish this part by actually looking at how to find your property, so hang in there for the fun stuff!

CHAPTER 8

Funding your purchase

You know why you are buying and which strategy you are going to use, but how are you going to finance your purchase? Simply getting a loan is not the solution. You need to work out what you can afford and how to access the funds. You also need to make sure the finance solution takes into account your needs today *and* tomorrow (this is where many people's finances fail to deliver).

The good old days when you could buy a property with no deposit are gone. Since the global financial crisis (GFC) lenders have reassessed their lending criteria. The new era of lending may appear tight, but banks are still keen to lend. They are just more particular about who they lend to. That does not mean it is easy, but it is not all that difficult either. You just need to position yourself as the ideal applicant so that you have the flexibility of choosing from lenders who have the right products to suit your needs.

What can you afford?

Most people are either limited by their borrowing capacity (which is based on their income and existing debts) or the funds they have to contribute. For the more advanced strategies, it's a mix of these and their experience.

So you need to know what your limitations are. The factor that affects most people is their ability to borrow — that is, the loan amount they are able to service — so let's look at that first.

Most investors are limited in the extent to which they can invest by their borrowing capacity. This can be, but is not necessarily, linked to how much you can afford (the GFC showed us what happens when people borrow more than they can afford). So for our purposes we're assuming you are a responsible investor who can afford the loan that the lender calculates you can.

But how do lenders calculate this?

How lenders assess you

You need to understand how lenders will assess you and why they might view you as a risk based on income, expenditure and other financial obligations such as credit cards and other loans.

Each lender will assess your financial position differently and their assessment of your borrowing capacity can vary by hundreds of thousands of dollars.

Consequently, you may need to vary your investment goals according to the lender who is most suited to your circumstances. Investing in what you can afford now and concentrating on good capital gain and income generation is going to provide you with a solid base from which to continue building an investment property portfolio. If you have equity in an existing property that you want to use to assist the purchase, you will need to do the number crunching described later in this chapter.

Regardless of whether you're an experienced investor or just getting into the market, it pays to do a little work beforehand to make sure you meet the lender's criteria and maximise your chances of a successful outcome. Lenders assess borrowing capacity using a range of criteria, which are subject to change, so be aware. In fact, keeping up with these changes is a full-time job, which is why more than 40 per cent (and this is increasing) of Australians use a professional mortgage broker. Not only do they save you time and often money but they get you the most appropriate loan for your needs.

The most common mistake people make is going back to their original lender, only to find out they can't borrow as much as they originally thought, and ending their enquiries there. Even worse, future purchases may be restricted because proper research wasn't undertaken to find the right product for their current circumstances. I have seen many investors limit their future investment opportunities by being short-sighted, sometimes over only a few dollars, and chasing low interest rates without looking at the big picture.

The new paradigm in a competitive market is that you should not be afraid to speak to several lenders; in fact it's a smart move. If you are looking at building a large portfolio, having your loans spread across various lenders with access to various policies is a good way of reducing your risk.

One of the most common traps people fall into when using only one lender is having that lender cross-collateralising their home with their investment property. Lenders often do this automatically, and you need to be aware if they are structuring your loan in this way. Read the contract, and if there is more than one property listed as a security, chances are you are cross-collaterised. In most cases it's not necessary. Lenders like it because it makes it harder for you to leave them in the future. Many borrowers like it because they believe it saves them on mortgage insurance costs. On the surface, using both securities to secure the new loan may not seem like a big deal. (Truth be told, if that is the limit of your portfolio, it probably won't be an issue.) However, if you plan to purchase more investment properties this structure could prevent you from growing your portfolio. As this does not affect everyone, you can access more information on my website at <www.yourpropertysuccessnow.com.au/ypsbookbonus>.

When it comes to determining your borrowing capacity there are a number of factors that lenders take into consideration, including the following.

$ What are your personal circumstances? This means your total monthly outgoings including all regular payments (for example, child care costs or gym memberships).

$ Do you have any additional funds that could contribute to the purchase? This could be savings, gifts or loans from a family member. Lenders will want to know the source of the funds and how long they have been in your account.

In addition, most lenders future-proof loans by factoring up their existing interest rate by up to 2 percentage points to protect you against future interest rate hikes.

It's good practice, when doing the numbers, to be conservative. You will hope that everything goes to plan, but despite best intentions this rarely happens; interest rates move, as do tenants and rents. You need to know what impact this will have on your borrowing capacity so you will need to choose the 'right' property to buy.

There are two critical numbers that will determine whether or not a lender will be willing to lend you money, and the amount they will be willing to lend. These are:

$ your net income, after allowing for all existing financial commitments

$ the amount you have saved that will form your deposit, or the value of any available equity that you have in other properties.

Serviceability

Lenders calculate your capacity to meet mortgage repayments — that is, your serviceability — by reviewing your numbers. Banks use the term 'serviceability', or borrowing capacity, to calculate your capacity to meet mortgage repayments. Essentially, this is what you earn and what you owe.

To responsibly maximise your borrowing capacity assessment, detail all your outgoing expenses. This should not be a 'guesstimate'. The best way is to look at bank statements as well as credit-card statements and list the outgoings over, say, a period of three months. You will need to ensure that all annual expenses, such as car registration and insurance premiums and any rates and taxes, are also factored in.

Lenders review what you earn, and they each have a different way of assessing your ability to service a loan. If you are a PAYG employee, proof of your consistent income over three pay periods will be required. If you have rental properties they will want the last rental statement. If you earn bonuses, commissions, receive government assistance, work in casual or part-time capacity or you are self-employed, they may or may not consider this income in full (depending on the lender). Self-employed applicants should be prepared to provide two full years of tax returns.

The final factor considered is the size of the deposit you have to put towards the purchase of the property, or the level of equity that you have in any other properties you own.

While lenders will lend up to 95 per cent LVR, this invariably comes with tight conditions, including lender's mortgage insurance (LMI). In some locations (for example, some rural locations) lenders will not lend more than 80 per cent, and for some property types (for example, one-bedroom apartments under 50 square metres in size) they will limit lending to 80 or even 70 per cent of market price.

The loan-to-value ratio (LVR) is a standard term used for assessing the loan amount as a percentage of the actual property value. It helps you to know how much you are contributing and how much the bank is contributing.

Now that you know what lenders will look at when assessing your borrowing capacity, it's time to find out how much you can actually afford to borrow.

Determining how much you can borrow

When it comes to determining your borrowing capacity, lenders only take into account your base salary, not your total salary package. This is because anything above the base salary is usually the superannuation contribution an employer makes on your behalf and is therefore not considered to be funds you can use to make loan repayments.

Be aware also that in most circumstances lenders will not include bonuses or commissions in their assessment of your income unless you can show a very consistent payment, say, over two or more years and even then they may give the amount a 'haircut' of 50 per cent.

Sounds confusing doesn't it? It needn't be. I will give you more details over the following pages.

Rental income

Lenders allow you to include the rental income you should earn from the property you are looking at buying. However, some will consider the average rental yield for the state or territory rather than the actual rent paid. For people looking at high yielding properties this is a disadvantage as the lender is not assessing their true ability to repay the loan. For new and existing properties, lenders base the rental income on 75 to 80 per cent (not 100 per cent) of the rental amount, to allow for on-costs, vacancies, and so on.

Living costs

Each lender has their own formula for calculating how much it costs you to live; this is their policy and it's not negotiable. Under the National Consumer Credit Protection Amendment Regulations introduced in January 2011, many lenders have decided that, to conservatively assess anyone's expenses, they will fall back on the *Henderson Poverty Index* figure as the lowest level of cost of living they will consider. However, the lender will request that you specify your actual expenses in order to determine whether or not you can afford the loan based on your current standard of living, so be prepared in case you have to provide them with a budget.

Credit cards are also a major factor that lenders consider in their assessment of your financial position. Every $5000 worth of credit limit (not balance) on your card means, on average, $20 000 less that you will be able to borrow.

Your credit file is the record kept on all the enquiries you have made for finance, be it your mobile phone account or previous mortgages. If you have not done this already, you should request your free copy of your credit file. Visit <www.yourpropertysuccessnow.com.au/ypsbookbonus> to find the providers of this file. You can pay to have it delivered straight to your inbox or get it for free by normal mail, which could take up to 10 days. Order it now.

The old rule of not spending more than you earn and investing what you save is a basic principle of financial management.

Affordability and gearing

Some lenders will also recognise the tax deductions you may be eligible for once you have purchased your investment property and they will add this to your income. After all, you can use your tax refund to help pay for your property.

 Toolbox tip

Astute investors don't wait until the end of the financial year. They get their tax return every pay. They do this by submitting a tax variation. Ask your accountant how to do this.

Your property will be either positively or negatively geared. Negative gearing is defined by the ATO as borrowing money to make an investment, where the interest and allowable deductions exceed the investment income and can be claimed as a deduction against other types of income.

This means that your borrowing costs exceed your investment income, which gives a tax benefit as Australian law allows you to deduct your borrowing costs from your total taxable income, provided that your investments are genuine. Some lenders will take this into account.

A property is positively geared when the total of the costs is lower than the rental income provided by the property before any tax concessions are taken into account.

A property is said to be positive cash flow if, when you add up the rental income and your personal annual income and deduct the holding costs (including depreciation) and the tax benefits you receive on the property, it moves from being negatively geared to positively geared. That is, the property is not classified as positive cash flow until the tax benefits are taken into account. However, positively geared property does not need the tax benefits to make it positive to hold.

These are all important considerations in the overall assessment of what you can afford. For investors in particular it is very important to distinguish between an investment property's net yield after tax and its cash costs after allowing for any tax variation. Some lenders take into account negative gearing benefits when assessing your affordability, so this is something that needs to be assessed carefully.

Borrowing capacity calculator

A mortgage broker can quickly determine your borrowing capacity with different lenders, advise how each one will assess you and then give you an idea of your the maximum amount you will be able to borrow before you submit a pre-approval. While getting pre-approval is smart, it only lasts for three months. So don't risk a hit on your credit file — only get a pre-approval when you are ready to act.

Toolbox tip

Each credit enquiry is recorded on your credit file. Lenders have a credit score they give each individual based on their loan application. This incorporates activity on your credit file, so only make an application for credit (that is, a loan application) when you are ready to use it.

Lenders have simple online 'borrowing capacity' calculators, so it's easy to get a rough guide of how much you could borrow. But be aware that this is only a very rough guide and does not mean you automatically qualify for that amount.

Be aware that lenders' policies change. This can happen overnight and may affect your purchase.

> ## Example
>
> In 2009 I assisted a client in buying her first home. She had $25 000 in savings to use as a deposit and with a 95 per cent LVR (a 5 per cent deposit) she could afford a $500 000 property. As the New South Wales government covered stamp duty for purchases of less than $500 000 she did not have to factor that into the equation. Hence she got pre-approval and went looking for a property.
>
> The bank, however, changed its policy, and the maximum LVR became 90 per cent. As a result, her $25 000 deposit was insufficient for a $500 000 property as she now had to come up with a 10 per cent deposit, which would have only permitted her to buy a $250 000 property. As you can see, her buying criteria for an inner-Sydney terrace house valued at $500 000 was no longer possible and she could now only afford a small unit in the outer western suburbs. It was looking as though she had wasted two months of property inspections—that is, if she stayed with the same lender. She changed lenders and could still purchase the $500 000 property.

So, being aware of lenders' policies and how they affect you and your buying criteria is important. Remember that there are many lenders—you just have to find the one that suits your needs.

Savings history

Regardless of the amount of your deposit, the most significant thing any lender will consider is the risk to them. From a lender's perspective it is becoming increasingly important that a potential borrower demonstrates a good overall savings history, which generally means genuine savings of 3 to 5 per cent of the property purchase price over three to six months. When assessing borrowing capacity, lenders will review your job stability; the stability in your living circumstances—that is, how often you move home—and most importantly, how much you earn in relation to how much you owe.

A good mortgage broker will be able to advise you on the level of savings each lender will ask you to demonstrate and over what time period.

'Opportunity' costs

Unless you have a 20 per cent deposit you will need to factor into your overall purchase costs the costs of lender's mortgage insurance (LMI). LMI is an insurance policy lenders take out to protect them—but they charge you. Many people hate the idea of LMI. However, I look at the cost of LMI from a different viewpoint: a 20 per cent deposit represents years of savings. Therefore, it is not uncommon for first-time purchasers to consider LMI as an 'opportunity' cost. In other words, it is a cost they are happy to pay for now if it means getting into the market sooner and building up equity in their property faster.

Property investors are also often prepared to buy with a higher LVR because they want to keep their funds available for future deposits and as a buffer. Extra funds will help them cover the difference between the income and cost of the property or may act as a buffer for the future.

Some investors look at their borrowing capacity and find they can borrow enough for two properties, but they only have enough savings for a 20 per cent deposit on one property. This is another reason why they may decide to pay LMI. Having more properties exposed to a growing market and taking into account compound growth could put you in a better position than having one property and waiting five years until you save enough for the next property. Remember also that that $250 000 property now would be worth $350 000 in five years' time if we apply a 7 per cent per annum interest rate. So you would have to save even more to have an acceptable amount of cash for a deposit. See how you could keep chasing your tail? LMI is an opportunity cost.

 Toolbox tip

It's important to note that LMI is the only cost that you can borrow and add to the loan amount. You can't borrow additional funds for fees or charges such as stamp duty, or for a renovation. If the lender says that they will lend 90 per cent of the property price, then that is it. You need to have some additional funds to contribute for those extra costs.

Understanding lenders is complex and ever changing but you need to be armed with your borrowing capacity so that you are not wasting your time looking at the wrong properties. Know how much you can afford so you can look at the areas where you can afford to buy.

This leads us to the next chapter: understanding how your borrowing capacity translates to a purchase price.

CHAPTER 9

Getting your loan approved

Once you know your borrowing capacity you then have to work out how this translates to a purchase price. You have to look at all the costs you need to cover, such as legal fees and stamp duty, which usually have to come from your savings. This is on top of what you need for the deposit. Many people make the mistake of thinking that their savings represent the deposit when in fact their savings need to cover both the deposit and the costs.

Consider this example of the costs in table 9.1 and see how they relate to the purchase price:

Table 9.1: example of costs

Savings	$20 000	
Stamp duty in WA (Note that stamp duty varies between states.)	–$15 700	
Legal fees and other fees and charges	–$2 000	
Total purchase costs	**–$17 700**	
Balance for deposit		$2 300

If you have $20 000 in savings and you want to buy a property worth $400 000, after all your costs you will have only $2 300 left over — or less than a 1 per cent deposit. Obviously in this case your savings are the limiting factor. The very most that lenders will consider lending is 95 per cent of the purchase price. You will need a deposit of at least 5 per cent — that is,

$20 000 — plus costs, which would come to $17 700. This means you will need $37 700 in savings.

The purchase price is often restricted by your contribution (savings towards a deposit) or your servicing capacity. Work out what your limitation is and what you can do to improve it. It might be getting rid of personal debt — for example, paying off credit cards — or it could be saving more. Keep in mind we are only talking about the funds needed to purchase the property. If you then decide you are going to do a renovation, or develop, or build a granny flat, you will need cash for that as well as the on-costs we discussed in chapter 6.

You could borrow the additional funds needed for building or developing — but usually only 80 per cent of the value of the work as stated in a fixed price builder's contract. However, if you were planning on managing your own renovation or building project, you would have to fund it yourself. Lenders usually only fund a construction or renovation that has a contract. This reduces their risk because having a professional managing the works means their money is protected. However, you may be able to access the funds from equity you have elsewhere.

Until recent times, it was common for people entering the property market for the first time to spend many years saving a deposit to buy a property. Others are fortunate enough to have someone help out or act as guarantor. However, if you are a smart investor, you will tap into your equity.

The equity model

This is the most common way for investors to access funds for their first property investment and it is usually from their home or their principal place of residence (PPOR). This model makes it possible for a borrower to unlock 'equity' from a property.

Releasing equity from your home in a structured way means you can keep your savings in the bank. Most investors want to combine the benefits of not using their own savings with tax minimisation advantages when buying an investment property. So keep in mind that you should be working through this with your experienced accountant and mortgage broker to get it right so that you can continue to invest.

Tapping into your equity

The best way to demonstrate how you can tap into the equity in your home is to use an example.

Example

Peta purchased her home some years ago for $200 000. She took out a loan for $160 000, using her savings of $50 000 to pay the deposit and costs (with an LVR of 80 per cent). The market value of the property is now $600 000. Her original loan of $160 000 has been reduced to $100 000 by making principal and interest repayments, and contributing her annual bonus.

To calculate the equity available in the property, Peta needs to decide how much equity to leave in. She wants the LVR to be no higher than 80 per cent (so that she doesn't incur lender's mortgage insurance).

The available equity is calculated as follows:

$$\$600\,000 \times 0.8 = \$480\,000$$

However, remember that Peta still has a $100 000 loan against her home, so we need to reduce the equity available by $100 000:

$$\$480\,000 - \$100\,000 = \$380\,000$$

She now has to determine how much she needs for the next purchase, as well as any additional funds she may need over the next five years for future investment. So, if her plan is to buy two investment properties in Victoria over the next five years worth $400 000 each using a 10 per cent deposit and she wants to complete a renovation on each property worth 10 per cent of the purchase price, the calculations would be as follows:

$$\text{Deposit: } \$400\#000 \times 10\% \times 2 = \$80\,000$$

Stamp duty and costs: $22 500 × 2 = $45 000 (stamp duty figures are calculated for Victoria, and allow $2500 for legal and associated costs)

$$\text{Renovation: } \$400\,000 \times 10\% \times 2 = \$80\,000$$

So Peta would need $205 000.

So, with $380 000 available in equity, Peta could consider getting approval to access the full $250 000 so that she has a buffer or a contingency in place. She will then have to contact her lender to ensure she can service all this new debt.

This example shows you the benefits of structuring your investments in a way that you can tap into your equity when you need it.

There are many different loan products—in fact, there are thousands. We are going to briefly look at the general lending terms so you can assess which type of product might suit your needs.

Understanding property finance

Most people see a loan in one dimension — that most loans have to be repaid within a certain period of time, usually 25 or 30 years. Now that you know how much you can borrow you need to choose the most appropriate loan product for your needs. This can be the difference between a property portfolio that grows and one that does not. As a mortgage broker I have dealt with many clients who have hit the 'servicing ceiling'. On review we often found that their initial finance structure was the one thing that had limited them in expanding their portfolio in later years. You need to understand not just your requirements today but look long term to what you want to achieve and make sure your structure will stand the test of time. So let's start at the beginning.

Types of loans

First of all you need to know the language of loans and finance. Following are examples of the more common loan types.

$ *Basic loan*. This is relatively inexpensive and inflexible. It is commonly used by an investor for the second or third property, to fit into an existing strategy where they don't need any bells and whistles.

$ *Variable-interest loan*. With this loan the interest rate reflects market fluctuations. This is the most common type of loan in Australia. There are often discounts on this type of loan based on the amount you borrow.

$ *Fixed-interest loan*. This is where the rate of interest is set for a period of time — usually three or five years — and it can't be changed during that period without high exit costs.

$ *Introductory low rate for a period*. This is often called the 'honeymoon' loan. It has a lower interest rate for a certain period of time (usually one year) and then a variable interest rate after that. This latter rate is usually the standard variable rate and has no associated discounts. Over the long term, this type of loan is generally more expensive.

$ *Split loan*. This is where one part of the loan has a fixed rate of interest and the rest has a variable interest rate. Basically, it gives you the best of both worlds as you're not exposed to your entire loan amount being charged at a higher rate should interest rates go up.

$ *Line of credit*. This resembles a transaction account where you are able to deposit and withdraw whatever amount you want (up to a specified limit), whenever you like. The interest is calculated on the daily balance. This is the most common way that people tap into their equity. It works like a big credit card. You pay interest on the amount you have drawn out, not the entire limit. This type of loan does not suit everyone, especially if you are a spender and you find having a large reserve of funds difficult to resist.

There are so many aspects you need to consider when looking at your loan requirements. It is certainly useful to have someone who does this every day, be it your lender or your mortgage broker, to help you.

However, although accountants, financial planners, mentors, brokers and lenders can assist you in setting up the right financial structure for your needs, you also have to take some responsibility by understanding your options and telling them what you require. Remember that knowledge is power, so don't be afraid to ask questions. If your lender is not prepared to set the loan up the way you want, then take your business elsewhere. You are the customer.

Some loans are set up in such a way that they not only restrict any negative gearing or structuring outcomes you had in mind, they can also be costly and greatly limit your ongoing property portfolio growth. From a taxation point of view, you only have one chance (in the eyes of the ATO) to get your initial loan set up correctly. You cannot go back and correct it later.

The basic considerations include:

$ principal and interest (P&I) loans versus interest only (IO) loans

$ interest rates

$ comparison rates

$ offset accounts

$ fixed-rate loans

$ lender's mortgage insurance (LMI)

$ professional packages

$ lender exposure.

There are other considerations but these are the main points you need to consider to ensure you choose a loan structure that is right for you.

Principal and interest or interest only?

Most people apply for a principal and interest (P&I) loan when they take out a home loan on their PPOR (principal place of residence) as they plan to own the property one day and want to pay it off by the end of the term. Fair enough. But this is not the mindset of smart investors. They use the property as a stepping stone to their financial goals; owning the property is not the end goal. Many new investors assume the P&I option is the only option they have. However, this is not the case. In fact, it is even an option for home owners.

If you have a 30-year standard variable loan, you should be aware that it is not until year 20 that you actually start paying off large portions of the original loan amount (the principal). In fact, in the first 20 years most of your monthly repayments are interest repayments, which means you have not built much equity (apart from the initial deposit) through your monthly mortgage repayments.

The average Australian moves home every seven to 12 years so the benefits of a P&I loan are questionable. Much depends on whether you consider your home as a stepping stone in your investment journey, or a home you will pay off.

Interest only is in your interest

Why do many property investors and many home owners only take out interest-only loans? Mainly because they don't plan to actually ever own the property. They just want to buy the right to use the property for its capital growth and rental yield. 'Huh?' I hear you saying.

Most people who buy an investment property already have a home loan or personal debt. In most cases it is in their interest (for taxation purposes) to put every spare dollar into paying off personal or non-deductible debt and maximising their investment or deductible debt. This is especially the case where the individual is using negative gearing as part of their strategy. Their aim is to have the largest claimable loan possible so they can claim interest deductions against it.

Investors who have a positively geared portfolio are more likely to consider the P&I loan for their investment, mainly because the lower the loan amount, the less interest they pay and the more positively geared the loan is. However, these people still usually only move to a P&I loan after they have paid off their home loan.

Interest rates

Mortgage interest rates are influenced by the cash rate set by the Reserve Bank of Australia (RBA). The lender adds a margin to this rate to cover their costs. As a result of increased competition, rates have moved around quite a bit outside the RBA cash rate. RBA rates can change month to month but more often than not stay fairly stable over any six-to-12-month period. Regardless, it is at the lender's discretion whether and when they pass on the RBA's official rate rise or reduction.

I once overheard someone say, 'I'm so glad I'm not with the RBA. They are always changing their interest rates'!

If the RBA increases interest rates by 0.25 per cent (known in the industry as '25 basis points') your lender may consider that their cost of acquiring funds has just increased and they will put rates up by 0.35 per cent. Similarly, they may not pass on all interest rate reductions to their clients.

Many unsuspecting buyers have entered into an agreement with lenders based on an attractive honeymoon rate, a basic loan or just an attractive general interest rate.

Focusing on the features of the loan product—not the interest rate—must be your priority.

Once you are satisfied that the features of a loan support your investment strategy and you proceed with the application process, then—and only then—should you factor in the interest rate.

This is especially relevant if you are using a renovation strategy. Your plan may be to do a renovation and then access the equity. This may be fine for the first six months while you're renovating because the lower interest rate is saving you money each month. However, as you opted for a lower interest rate rather than checking that the loan features support your strategy, you may have neglected to find out other important details. Perhaps the lender will not allow you to access equity through a line of credit, or you're required to pay an additional $500 switching fee (so much for the money you saved), or you have to pay an application fee to take out a more suitable loan, or—worse still—you are up for bank costs because you have to go to another lender.

Bottom line? Focusing only on the interest rate is a naive way to assess which product is right for your strategy. It is for this reason that I rarely deal with clients who are looking only for the cheapest interest rate — it tells me they aren't smart investors with a long-term investment strategy.

Comparison rates

The comparison rate is a calculation that includes the interest rate advertised on the day and any set-up fees such as establishment fees, legal and valuation fees and ongoing account fees. This may be calculated over various time periods, although 25 years is generally the accepted time period.

Comparison rates are handy as they help the borrower get a feel for the total cost of the loan and, as the name suggests, help you compare loan products across lenders.

This is most important for anyone who might be tempted to consider what are known as 'honeymoon' rates, which usually revert to a much higher interest rate at the end of the first 12 months. The comparison rate assists you in readily assessing just how much of a saving (or not) you may be making.

However, the features of a loan are not part of the comparison rate. So if you want an offset account, for example, which could save you thousands of dollars and years off your loan, be aware that this feature will not be included in the comparison rate.

Offset accounts

One of the things you should consider when deciding on the loan that's best for you is the benefit of an offset account, which comes with many 'professional' loan packages.

An offset account is essentially a savings account — not a loan account — that is linked to your loan. It offsets your loan. This means that any balance you have in your offset account reduces the interest you pay on your interest-only loan. This is one of the most useful loan features any investor can have.

Let's look at how an offset account works.

Example

Ivan puts $35000 in an offset account to offset a $315000 interest-only loan. The bank then deducts the funds in the savings offset account ($35000) from the loan amount of $315000 and only charges him interest on the balance ($280000).

The above example is for an interest-only (IO) loan. The offset works differently for principal and interest (P&I) loans. In this case, the savings you make are attributed to the term of the loan, effectively reducing the term of the loan, while your monthly repayments stay the same or are reduced to reflect the lower interest payment you will make over the long term.

Mostly, offset accounts are placed on a variable loan against a home. They assist in reducing the term of the loan and thereby the overall interest you have to pay.

Essentially, you deposit your salary and savings into the offset account each month and when the interest is calculated daily (charged monthly) those additional funds will help to further reduce your monthly loan repayment, thus improving your monthly cash flow.

If you have a redraw facility (rather than an offset account) against an investment property, you need to be aware that if you use the funds for personal use—be it for your next home, car or family holiday—the portion of the interest on that redrawn amount of the loan will not be tax deductible. However, if the funds are in an offset account against an investment property—such as a savings account—you can use them whenever you want for whatever you want and the original loan amount will not be affected.

Fixed-rate loans

Be aware that you can only fix a standard variable loan for the amount of the original loan. That is, you cannot fix a line of credit as the balance can fluctuate and the lender is unable to calculate a loan repayment on this basis.

Essentially, fixing a loan has many benefits—especially the 'I can sleep at night' factor. With a fixed loan you know what you are committed to repay for a set period of time. You just have to live with the consequences if the rates go down.

History shows that the economists employed by the banks to work out how the bank can make money usually get it right. Hence, over the past

20 years there have only been a handful of times when fixed-rate loans have outperformed the variable rate of the day.

Over the long term, interest rates average about 7.5 per cent. Borrowers who locked in at more than 9 per cent in 2008 found that when rates dropped in 2009 their break costs were exorbitant. So you need to be aware of the consequences in case you have to break the fixed-rate loan contract (for example, if you sell the property).

Lender's mortgage insurance (LMI)

A deposit of less than 20 per cent means you will incur lender's mortgage insurance (LMI) on your loan. LMI protects the bank (not you) in case you default. In most cases, lenders will make it easier for you by allowing you to add the one-off premium cost of the LMI to your loan so that you don't have to take it from your savings.

Each lender has different premium rates for LMI. As the loan amount increases and the loan-to-value ratio (LVR) increases, so too will the LMI premium.

LMI can be seen in two ways. On the one hand it can be perceived as wasted money. On the other hand it can be viewed as merely an 'opportunity' cost (as discussed in chapter 8). Often, investors choose to pay a lower deposit (for example, 5 or 10 per cent) and pay LMI so they can keep the remaining money in savings or equity for their next purchase.

You need to decide which approach is right for you. There can also be tax benefits to consider. If you are paying the LMI from your own pocket for an investment property, this can be classed as a borrowing expense and is then deductible as a borrowing expense. If you choose to add the LMI premium to the loan you can claim this as a 'cost' in your tax return.

Another situation where you can consider LMI as an 'opportunity' cost is when you want to be very aggressive with your investment portfolio and buy many properties. You may choose to spread a finite amount of savings or equity over a number of purchases by taking out several loans with lower deposits, thus incurring LMI.

Professional packages

Years ago 'professional packages' were only offered to a few borrowers in elite professions. These days anyone who borrows more than $150 000 can find themselves a professional package. Essentially, a professional package waives the application fees, which are usually between $600 and $750, the valuation fees (typically about $250), monthly account fees of $10, as well as fees for the associated savings account (which could be another $10 per month). Instead institutions charge one annual fee of between $120 and $400, depending on the lender (this could also be spread out as a monthly fee).

Each lender also has additional benefits associated with its professional package — for example, fee-free credit cards and discounts on insurance. The biggest benefit of a professional package is the discount, which is generally 0.7 per cent off the standard variable rate (or more if you borrow more than $250000). This often results in the same interest rate as the lender's basic product but with all the bells and whistles. While there can be thousands of dollars of benefit for the annual fee payment, the biggest benefit of professional packages is the fee-free offset accounts and the fact that you can include future properties in your portfolio for the same annual fee, which saves you money.

Lender exposure

As you begin to build up an investment portfolio, there's a lot to be said for spreading the risk over several different lenders. Normally I suggest using a professional package for a home purchase as this allows some scope for tapping into the equity using an additional loan such as a line of credit (LOC), which will cover your purchasing goals for up to five years, as we discussed in chapter 8. Then future investment property purchases may also be included under the original professional package and the offset account is usually free.

However, I would urge you to consider capping your borrowings with any one lender to about $800000. Once you get to $1 million in lending with any one lender they will look at you differently because they'll apply a different risk profile to you, potentially making it harder for you to borrow with them in future. However, at $800000 you'll still have room for a few top-ups should you need to extend existing loans in future years. While this may seem like a lot of unnecessary work, structuring your loans so they are flexible and separate (that is, not cross-collateralised) will get you where you want to be sooner.

Knowing the language of finance will assist you in understanding what lenders are offering you so you can work out whether it fits your requirements. Many people don't understand the process of lending: what all the different stages mean and when your loan is actually approved. For further clarification go to <www.yourpropertysuccessnow.com.au/ypsbookbonus> to learn about this process. There has been many a surprised borrower who thought that the pre-approval they had from the bank meant the lender was actually going to lend the funds for any property they were planning on buying. It is not until you have formal, unconditional approval that you should breathe easy. Having said that, after getting formal approval on my first purchase one of the 'big four' banks decided they didn't want to proceed as my borrower profile no longer matched their lending profile and they wouldn't lend me 95 per cent. This meant that two weeks before settlement I had to rush around to source a new lender.

Professional help

Obviously, in a situation like the one I just described, having a mortgage broker who could assist me in getting another lender quickly was invaluable. I just didn't have the time or knowledge to undertake that myself. There are many professionals who can assist you on your property investing journey.

These professionals include:

$ a financial planner

$ an accountant

$ a mortgage broker

$ a buyer's agent

$ a valuer

$ a quantity surveyor

$ a rental manager

$ an architect

$ an interior designer

$ pest and building inspectors.

You may not need the services of all of these professionals. On the other hand, this list is not exhaustive.

There are questions that you should ask professionals and qualifications that they should have. For a checklist of questions and qualifications for each professional visit my website at <www.yourpropertysuccessnow.com.au/ypsbookbonus>.

CHAPTER 10

Locating a property

As an investor you'll want to combine your property investing strategy and your buying criteria, and have a toolkit of websites and other tools to help you limit the number of properties and buying locations on your list so that you can achieve your financial goals in the time frame you've set for yourself. Sounds simple doesn't it? Well, it's not quite that easy.

Unfortunately, buying the perfect property that outperforms the market is not easy. If it were, anyone with a bit of extra cash would become rich by investing in real estate. Locating a property builds on what you've already learned. Making it work for you means running the numbers, doing the research and knowing exactly what you're after.

In this chapter I will show how you can start with the big picture and work your way down to an actual property. You have already defined your strategy and your buying criteria. Therefore, you should have a pretty good idea of what to look for and where you are going to look. For example, your specific buying criteria for locating your property may be that it will cost less than $400 000 in an area that should achieve 7 per cent per annum capital growth and 5 per cent per annum rental yield and give you the opportunity to renovate with a 10 per cent renovation cost and a 15 per cent profit.

By undertaking this step alone you have already narrowed down the huge number of suburbs and towns in Australia to a few hundred that could satisfy your requirements. (In fact, Residex has defined 8300 suburbs and towns with houses in Australia and another 3800 containing units, making a total of more than 12 000.) Now we just need to get those few hundred down to about three so you can do the real research necessary for finding the property that will suit your needs and help you to build your portfolio.

If we look at past property performance we know that a well-located house or unit can double in value every seven to 10 years. As an astute investor, your job is to find a property that will consistently outperform other properties in the same area, as well as exceeding the rate of inflation by at least 3 to 5 percentage points. If you've made the right moves — understanding your goal and the time frame you are working within, your property investing strategy, your buying criteria and the location that will enable you to achieve your goals — you will be 'firing' on all cylinders.

Performance factors

The big picture is to look at the factors that influence the long-term performance of a property and overlay them with your personal requirements. Those factors are:

$ capital growth — buying where people want to live

$ rental yield — cash flow for maintaining your portfolio

$ scarcity.

Let's look at each of these.

Capital growth

Property prices are always higher closer to the centre of a city because the centre is where people want to be for work or lifestyle — and they are prepared to pay for it. Think about it this way: if you draw a circle with a radius of, say, 25 kilometres from the centre of any capital city, you will have hundreds of suburbs to search. Once you draw circles within say 10 or 12 kilometres you have narrowed the search to a few dozen suburbs. Even if you go 15 kilometres out of Sydney's CBD — where there are many amenities that will appeal to renters and future owner-occupiers — you have a finite search field.

This information is just as relevant if you are considering looking in a regional town. Growing up in Dubbo, I remember being shocked in Grade 3 when I heard several students had never been across the bridge separating Dubbo's suburbs. So just because a town may have a population of 30 000 and one postcode, don't think that every part of the town is equally popular in terms of people wanting to live there; for example, it's likely many people will want to live near a shopping centre.

Toolbox tip

When looking at an area to assess, make sure you also look at the rental properties in the area. If you see advertisements that say, 'on the right side of the highway', or 'in the dress circle precinct' then you know that there are areas within your area that you need to consider. If a real estate agent has made the effort to point this out, listen!

It's a kind of 'golden rule' when buying property that the smaller the city, the closer in you should go to the CBD as people will always want to live close to the centre. There's a convenience factor and a demand factor that underpin the opportunity for capital gain. In real estate circles, suburbs 5 and 10 kilometres from the centre of the CBD are referred to as 'inner ring' suburbs. Those within 5 kilometres are CBD ring suburbs. CBD ring suburbs will over time bring even higher rental returns for investors, although the price of such properties could be prohibitive, with the exception, perhaps, of apartments. It is important to note that outer suburbs have outperformed many inner-ring suburbs based on capital growth percentages. This is mainly due to affordability issues. Many positively geared property portfolios are built in outer-ring suburbs of the capital cities or in regional areas.

Rental yield
This is important. Capital growth will enable you to tap into equity to build your portfolio and allow you to reach a point where you can sell up and live your dreams, but rental return will enable you to hold and build your portfolio. You need both.

Scarcity
Some investors look for what is referred to as the 'scarcity' factor. This is when a property has a valuable attribute, such as a wonderful view, being located near a golf course or having heritage features. For optimal returns in both capital gains and yield, investors should stick to properties that are scarce or have scarce characteristics, such as older houses in inner suburbs, but unfortunately they are not in abundant supply.

Deciding where to buy

Applying a low-risk approach to your endeavour is crucial for long-term sustained success. As we have already discussed, the vast majority of property investors in Australia only have one investment property. Many investors bought without much research and were genuinely surprised when the property investing fad that was making everyone else rich didn't work for them.

You'll need to remember to avoid buying based on emotion; investing is about the numbers and the research. Don't fall prey to the 'gorgeous cottage' down the street. As I alluded to earlier, take care of gross claims of 'bargains' and avoid supposed 'hot spots', unless you have done your own research.

By the time you read about hot spots in the paper or overhear talk about the most recent bargain property, the opportunity has probably expired. Information you get, at least as a new investor, is probably already three to six months old. Go ahead and take a peek if you must, but avoid wasting your time on 'sure things' or 'golden opportunities'. Let's be serious: if it sounds too good to be true, it probably is.

You need to focus on three things:

$ why you are buying

$ where to buy

$ how to buy.

Everything else is secondary, and guess what? You will be the one finding the hot spots!

Finding hot spots

One of the prongs of the Trident Strategy is buying in high-growth areas. So how do you find areas that will outperform the market? First take note of what we covered earlier in the chapter: buy where people want to (and need to) live as this creates demand. Recognise what they want and anticipate where they will have to live to fit their budget. This is equally true for buying in cities or regional areas.

My personal criteria are to buy in inner-ring suburbs where demand for rental property is high; buy in good streets (safe, close to transport and well kept);

and, if buying an apartment, buy in a small, old-style building where there is a significant land component (and potential to renovate).

Let's look at these two factors: buying where people want and need to live, and finding good capital growth areas.

The ripple effect

Let's think of where people aspire to live. Think of the 'good' areas in your home town or suburb. What characteristics do they have? The issue is, these areas are usually outside your price range, and they may have already been through their growth phase. So how do you find an area that you can afford and an area where people want to live? Basically, you apply your buying criteria. What you will find is that some suburbs may not have all the characteristics you're looking for in an ideal investment property . . . yet.

The most promising properties are usually located in suburbs that are part of the ripple effect; that is, suburbs bordering an area that has had high growth but the surrounding areas have not taken off yet. Or, they are suburbs where some degree of gentrification or council and local business initiatives are improving the area.

Your job is to research and find the areas while they are affordable and before everyone else finds them, then hold on while you ride the capital growth wave.

Growth drivers

Sudden changes in capital growth are usually the result of a single factor. This could be new legislation, infrastructure changes, the 'x' factor, planning or rezoning or a new industry.

State and local government planning changes can move the goal posts quickly. One example is the New South Wales 2009 planning changes, which included a regulation allowing a 60-square-metre second dwelling to be built on land sizes of more than 450 square metres without a lot of paperwork. This has created growth in areas with properties that lend themselves to this strategy: quick, substantial and transient population growth.

You may have noticed that lower priced areas within commutable distances from the CBD shot up in value when the Australian government announced the First

Home Buyers Grant of $14000. Or that the substantial change in population growth in Mt Barker, South Australia, which occurred between the 2001 and 2006 census, was a result of the area becoming more commutable due to new roads that connected it to the city, hence cutting travel times. You should also see changes in population growth when an area is rezoned as residential.

It pays to keep an eye on where the big companies are opening new stores. You can bet Coles knows something about the population demands of an area if they have committed to opening a new store.

For the 'x' factor you have to be very observant. In recent years, for example, the My School website, which rates schools, was introduced. The best performing high schools generally only take students from their catchment areas; that is, from specific suburbs. So guess which suburbs went up in value? Hence, a property on one side of the street — outside the catchment zone — would not experience as much growth as one on the other side of the street — within the catchment zone.

Refining your list

To dig into the finding-a-property market, you'll need to be able to complete 90 per cent of your research and analysis at home before you pound the streets looking for the best deal. When you do finally leave home, you'll be armed with your own customised checklist, which will serve as a reminder of what you are looking for. If a property does not meet the criteria you've set for yourself, pass it by ... yes, really!

Making sure that your goals are aligned with reality will virtually take the risk out of investing. Sure, we all dream of waking up rich — it's like winning the lottery. But real estate investing is a get-rich-slow kind of scheme. The good news is that if you get it right you do get rich.

 Toolbox tip

You do need to double check that the property you are buying looks like all the other properties on the market in the price range you are looking at. In other words, if you are looking at a $300 000 property in an area where the median property is a three-bedroom house and your

$300 000 property is a one-bedroom house with a small office, you are not buying a median property. Make sure you know the median price and what the median property looks like. Once you've done that, you'll need to know the characteristics of the average person who wants to live in the median property. That's the demographics (we looked at demographics briefly in chapter 7 and we'll discuss it in more depth shortly).

In the previous chapter we discussed how to work out how much you can borrow. Combined with your goals and strategy, with this information you can work out a purchase price that best suits your needs. For example, if you can afford to buy a property worth $900 000, you might consider three $300 000 properties in different locations. The trick here is not to base your budget on anyone else's criteria, just yours. So don't get excited if a lender tells you your borrowing capacity is a lot higher — stick to your buying criteria.

Toolbox tip

If your buying criteria is to purchase a property worth $400 000, look at areas with median prices of 15 to 20 per cent above this as well. You never know what your negotiation skills or someone's circumstances might deliver you. However, the higher you go in price, the less chance you have of buying a property below market value—one of the prongs of the Trident Strategy.

You don't want to overestimate your purchasing or investing power. Finding how your numbers fit into the median of any given area will require a bit of research. So, being able to afford a $900 000 property does not mean you start with areas where the median is that amount. You need to go back to your buying criteria. You have already worked out what price range you should target so that is the only median price you should look at.

Narrowing your areas

To conduct your research, you need to know what the median prices are for areas. You can do this with minimum outlay by going to a newsagency and getting a copy of *Smart Property Investment*, *Your Investment Property*, or *Australian Property Investor* magazines.

Toolbox tip

For the best research results, buy all three magazines. Each of these magazines uses a different data source, so you'll have the best information if you combine the data of all three. In the back of each of these publications is a handy little section that contains data on every suburb in Australia. This data includes median values, rental yield and past growth, as well as average time on the market. This is crucial information for investors and can help you nail down which suburb to target, what to expect to pay, the potential profit, and more.

Check out the main real estate websites for this information. However, although they do give good suburb data you need to know which suburbs to search, whereas the magazines list every suburb and town.

Toolbox tip

Make sure you note down the name of the magazine from which you obtain the data for median values, rental yield and past growth, as well as average time on the market as you will need this information later when you are doing comparisons (so that you know you are comparing apples with apples). The strange thing is that each major provider of property statistics calculates median prices differently and as such they all have different results.

Start by listing all the suburbs you can afford and add 10 per cent to allow some room for negotiation (the magazines also show past growth and rental yield so you can remove those areas that do not fit your buying criteria). You still might have a long list, so apply your buying criteria again. Now limit yourself to a particular state, a town of a particular size, an area a certain distance from a CBD.

Toolbox tip

When arriving at your final three suburbs it's a good idea to have them within 5 to 8 kilometres of each other for two main reasons: this makes it manageable when doing inspections and you will find that the demographics remain consistent or vary little. For example, the property type you are targeting and the type of tenant you are attracting will be similar. The demographic within that range will not change a lot, so within that radius your target demographic tenant may be a family with kids requiring a three-bedroom house and a garage, whereas 25 kilometres away the renter may be a single person preferring an apartment close to transport.

Now it's time to start getting to know these areas intimately so that you can narrow your list down to about three properties — a manageable number to physically inspect.

Culling your list

How do you start culling to reduce the number of areas on your list? This is where you need to look at many variables so you can discard those areas, suburbs or towns that do not fit.

Positive population growth

You're looking here for information on industries coming to the area or major changes to the area. Surprisingly, council websites have most of this information available for free with their projections for infrastructure based on future population requirements. You need to make sure that population growth fundamentals do in fact exist; for example, a new hospital, a new port facility, a new Westfield shopping centre. After all, if growth is being led by a baby boom, there won't be as many new houses needed as there would be if the growth is due to a new industry in town.

Rental demand

First, start looking on real estate websites to see how many properties are on the market for sale. Then check how many are listed for rent. After all, if there is a glut of rental properties you may have difficulty renting yours out. High rental demand is a function of population demand. Be aware though that in an area with new developments there will be capital growth and new owner-occupiers moving into the area so there may be a low demand for rental accommodation.

Supply

Look for information on new developments in the areas you're interested in. You should find this on council websites in their approvals area. If you're considering buying a unit and there are 1600 new units hitting the market over the coming year, reducing demand for rental properties, you want to know about it. Having a limited supply of properties in the area ensures demand remains strong. Check for council rulings that limit the construction of high-rise unit developments. This can affect the supply-and-demand equilibrium and even create a market for older-style units.

Good past growth

We can only really use the past to help us predict the future (no guarantees of course!). Property magazines such as *Australian Property Investor* track and publish the capital growth of suburbs over the past 10, five, three and one years. (Periods of less than one year can be heavily influenced by abnormalities of the market.) It would be an even better indication of past capital growth if you can access the past 20 years of annual growth rates. However, you would have to pay for reports on these. (The annual supplement with the Residex report gives this information.) If you notice that there has been little capital growth in a suburb compared to the areas or suburbs surrounding it, you may have found a hot spot. If the surrounding suburbs have had little growth, it may be an indication that there is not enough demand to drive capital growth.

Good future growth

This is harder to find. You could look at reports that identify many suburbs and towns in an individual state. However, these usually cost more than $150. You can use websites such as <www.residex.com.au> and buy suburb reports, which cost about ninety dollars each, that predict future growth. However, if you need reports on 10 properties in 10 different suburbs they can become expensive. Ask your mortgage broker if they will provide them for you. The experts who write the reports look at population changes, council plans and infrastructure announcements before making their assessments. The Ryder report produced by <www.hotspotting.com.au> is one such report that goes into a huge amount of detail on this type of information.

Toolbox tip

When growing your portfolio, vary your property locations across several states. This gives you access to a larger portfolio value before you have to pay land tax as every state has its own threshold of land value that has to be reached before you have to start paying land tax (this may change in the future). There are many benefits to spreading your properties between states, because you can access equity when the market is booming in one state but flat in another.

You should now be able to narrow down your list of eight to 10 areas to about three. More than this becomes too hard to not only research in detail, but also to truly be able to monitor and inspect.

Getting to know suburbs

You should now familiarise yourself with the suburbs you've selected and test their suitability to your own individual strategy. Once you know everything about them intimately you will be able to identify the best of the bunch.

Why should you assess them to your buying criteria? Because, although it may sound beneficial to have a huge number of properties from which to choose, in reality having too many properties can make things confusing and difficult to manage. Narrowing the pool of possibilities helps you manage your expectations and efficiently target specific properties.

Toolbox tip

Set up an alert with a property website for rental properties in your selected area using your criteria (for example, a three-bedroom house

Toolbox tip (*cont'd*)

with a garage). Every time a property appears that matches your criteria you will be notified. You can monitor not just the competition and the asking price, but check out what the property features are and how quickly they are renting. You'll soon find out what renters want.

Is it smarter to sink your cash into an older property that can be improved via renovations, or a new property that delivers instant high tax incentives? There are advantages and disadvantages of both types of investment, but ultimately it depends on your own strategy, goals and buying criteria.

Toolbox tip

On a personal note, as we own so many properties in New South Wales our land tax bill has been more than $15000 per annum in recent years. This cost can greatly reduce your cash flow and even turn a positively geared property into a negatively geared one. For bonus material, visit <www.yourpropertysuccessnow.com.au/ypsbookbonus> to get up-to-date information on thresholds in each state and the latest position on the federal-based payment.

As an investor you can claim depreciation on all items that qualify under ATO rules. These include many fixtures and fittings, such as blinds and dishwashers. Newer properties offer a higher rate of depreciation than older properties.

If you buy an older property, you should investigate the prices in the area and compare these against the property's asking price and the median price for the area. The opportunity to add value to an older home can be an advantage as this can build equity if you are smart with you renovation. Remember the Trident Strategy prongs: renovation helps you create equity in the medium term.

A low-maintenance property—well built and free from defects—equals fewer out-of-pocket expenses for you.

Sometimes, older homes have features that newer homes simply don't offer—such as beautiful cornices or period features—but it is the location that is of paramount importance and that the property fits with the area. Many older suburbs have a tree-lined charm and appeal that may not be available in dense inner-city suburbs, which have demand from purchasers as well as tenants. So consider the advantages of being able to add equity through renovation and possibly make tens of thousands of dollars against the benefit of the tax depreciation for a new house, which could save you $10 000 per year. The equity gained through a renovation has a cumulative effect: it increases in a compound fashion—so $25 000 spent now may result in $50 000 in equity in seven years' time—whereas the depreciation benefit will reduce as the years mount up.

Visit <www.yourpropertysuccessnow.com.au/ypsbookbonus> to access a depreciation calculator so you can see what you can claim against your taxable income.

Selecting suburbs

It's now time to reassess the suburbs you have selected against your buying criteria. Check that they match:

$ the yield that you require

$ the predicted future growth that you want

$ the supply and demand (what is driving demand and is there a shortage of properties?)

$ the price range.

There is also another dimension you need to assess before you start looking for the actual property. You need to consider now the demographics of the areas you have selected.

CHAPTER 11

Knowing your demographics

I'm going to confess that I can get lost in demographic information for hours. I love it! I really find it an interesting challenge to be able to work out what a typical household looks like and translate that into what a typical property suited to that tenant should look like.

Keep in mind that from the previous chapter we know the median for an area and together with what we know from researching real estate sales websites, we also have an idea about what that typical property looks like (for example, a three-bedroom weatherboard house or a two-bedroom brick house).

Now let's take it a step further. Many of the real estate sales websites offer suburb profiles (or similar information). The information produced in the suburb profiles is sourced from the Australian Bureau of Statistics (that is, census data) and gives you an idea about what a suburb or town looks like.

Let's assume I have never been to postcode 2032 in Sydney. Have a look at the demographic information in table 11.1 and tell me what strikes you about what you see.

Table 11.1: the demographics of postcode 2032

Demographics		
Population size	**Postcode: 2032**	**Region: Sydney**
All people	14 976	4 095 244
Country of origin	**Postcode: 2032**	**Region: Sydney**
Australian born	44 per cent	60 per cent

(continued)

Table 11.1: the demographics of postcode 2032 (*cont'd*)

Born overseas—top 5	Postcode: 2032	Region: Sydney
China	6 per cent	2 per cent
Indonesia	5 per cent	0 per cent
Greece	3 per cent	0 per cent
Hong Kong	3 per cent	0 per cent
Malaysia	2 per cent	0 per cent
Age statistics	**Postcode: 2032**	**Region: Sydney**
20–39	39 per cent	30 per cent
40–59	23 per cent	26 per cent
60+	17 per cent	16 per cent
5–19	15 per cent	19 per cent
0–4	5 per cent	6 per cent
Family statistics—top 5	**Postcode: 2032**	**Region: Sydney**
Never married	46 per cent	34 per cent
Married	39 per cent	49 per cent
Divorced	6 per cent	7 per cent
Widowed	5 per cent	5 per cent
Separated	2 per cent	2 per cent
Religion—top 5	**Postcode: 2032**	**Region: Sydney**
Catholic	25 per cent	29 per cent
No religion	17 per cent	14 per cent
Other	13 per cent	10 per cent
Eastern Orthodox	12 per cent	4 per cent
Anglican	9 per cent	17 per cent
Occupation—top 5	**Postcode: 2032**	**Region: Sydney**
Health care and social assistance	11 per cent	9 per cent
Professional/scientific and technical services	10 per cent	8 per cent
Retail trade	10 per cent	10 per cent
Accommodation and food services	9 per cent	6 per cent
Education and training	9 per cent	7 per cent
Education—top 5	**Postcode: 2032**	**Region: Sydney**
Not attending (working)	51 per cent	58 per cent
University or other tertiary institution	18 per cent	5 per cent

Infants/primary	6 per cent	10 per cent
Secondary education	5 per cent	8 per cent
Technical or further education	2 per cent	3 per cent
Transport to work—top 5	**Postcode: 2032**	**Region: Sydney**
Car (driver)	40 per cent	53 per cent
Bus only	23 per cent	4 per cent
Walk	8 per cent	4 per cent
Car (passenger)	5 per cent	5 per cent
Train and other	3 per cent	4 per cent
Type of dwelling—top 3	**Postcode: 2032**	**Region: Sydney**
Separate house	42 per cent	71 per cent
Semi/terrace	40 per cent	21 per cent
Flat	36 per cent	17 per cent
Nature of occupancy—top 3	**Postcode: 2032**	**Region: Sydney**
Rented	47 per cent	31 per cent
Fully owned	30 per cent	31 per cent
Purchasing	17 per cent	33 per cent
Monthly loan repayment—top 3	**Postcode: 2032**	**Region: Sydney**
$1600+	61 per cent	54 per cent
$950–$1199	7 per cent	8 per cent
$1400–$1599	5 per cent	7 per cent

Note: Where the demographics are shown as a ranking (rather than the actual demographic) the number indicates the ranking from most common to less common. The rank in the Comparison Region indicates where the demographic of the Target Region ranks in the Comparison Region.

Source: Australian Property Monitors Home Price Guide <www.homepriceguide.com.au>

Here's what strikes me about this specific example (this should help you to apply this type of thinking to your selected suburbs):

$ *Nationality.* A high proportion of residents in the area are of Indonesian, Chinese and Greek nationality. So, I may start making some general notes on what type of accommodation these nationalities could prefer. For example, I would heighten my attention on units for the Asian population, so I would note down to keep that in mind.

$ *Age of the population.* This tells me that, compared to the rest of Sydney, a large proportion of the population is in the 20- to 39-year-old age group. I would start wondering if I was near a tertiary learning institution such as a university. This might also fit with the nationality data. If I found a high proportion of school-age children, I would note down that I want to know where the schools are located with respect to any property I am considering, and if I wanted to be more thorough, I would look at the My School website at <www.myschool.edu.au> and see which schools in the area are better than others.

$ *Marital status.* The demographic tells me that there is a large percentage — 46 per cent in fact — of single people living in the area. Now I might start thinking that university accommodation is something I need to consider if I'm going to invest here. Also, I might consider one- or two-bedroom accommodation for students, not five-bedroom houses.

$ *Education.* Wow! Almost four times as many people in this suburb are at university than in all of Sydney. This information is really starting to indicate some important criteria to consider when looking at purchasing an investment property in this area.

$ *Transport to work.* This data informs me that compared with all the people in Sydney, five times as many people in this suburb travel on public transport. So, straight away, I start thinking that a garage may not be that important. However, I would want the property I buy to be within 300 metres of the bus or train station.

$ *Type of dwelling.* Just to confirm my suspicions, a large proportion of the population of this area lives in units or semis, so that is the typical type of property for most people in the area.

$ *Nature of occupancy.* And just in case I missed it completely, this information tells me that a very large proportion of individuals in this area are renting. As an investor, I know this means that people want to live here. From what I have learned above, I know that they need to live here because it is close to a university or other tertiary learning institution.

Drivers of population growth and sustainable rental demand are often found around hospitals, universities and transport hubs.

So, what have I learned about this postcode? I know that most people rent units and semis and catch public transport, and a large proportion are single and may be from overseas. Now that I have a picture of what my potential tenant looks like, I can start working out what kind of property I need; that is, a two-bedroom unit or semi without a carport or garage that is within walking distance of either the university or public transport. In addition, I may even consider a furnished property geared towards overseas students as I could then charge a higher rent and convert a property within my price range into a rental property that offers higher than normal yield for that area.

Toolbox tip

People will interpret information differently. At the end of the day the numbers don't lie. Bernard Salt from KPMG is one of Australia's most well-known commentators on demographics—in fact, he has written many books on the topic. To learn how to start reading the numbers check out some of his articles. He has a number of best-selling books and writes for *The Australian*.

You may be wondering why I would look at a two-bedroom unit for a single person. Well, often people who want to live alone also want an office. Also, I am minimising my risk by having a two-bedroom unit as I not only cater for my target market — that is, people living alone — but also couples, flatmates or even a family with one child. Remember plan B: always anticipate the potential risk and minimise it. All the information is there; you just need to interpret it.

Example

At one stage after moving from Melbourne to Sydney, when both my husband and I were looking at buying a property, we had our list of three suburbs each. Unfortunately our buying criteria and purchase prices differed. So on Saturdays we had what amounted to a military campaign of inspections involving flying across the Sydney Harbour Bridge and paying its tolls at least five times to cover Maroubra, Manly, Mosman, Newtown, Balmain and Bondi.

We still managed to see more than 10 properties a day but as you can imagine we only spent on average seven minutes at each property. (Incidentally, that's about the same amount of time a bank-organised valuer will spend at your property.) Once you know what you're looking for . . . well, you know what you're looking for. With five minutes for some inspections you can imagine how important a checklist becomes for recording what you see, even as a mental trigger of what to look for.

Information is power and it is the foundation of sound decision making. For instance, if you're looking at a property to turn over and sell quickly in an area where most people rent, you're probably barking up the wrong tree. Remember that more than 65 per cent of properties are owner occupied so if you are looking at an area that has a high proportion of renters you may find that a quick flip can be difficult if you are targeting investors, as you have already extracted the value. For a flipping strategy you may be better to target areas with higher proportions of owner occupiers who want the dream house now.

Conversely, this might be an area where other investors want to buy, so knowing who is your future potential buyer is also important. That way, as a fall-back plan, if you need to sell quickly you want your property to be attractive to the largest market available. If the area has a high proportion of renters, then investors will also be interested in buying your property. The key is to make the property attractive to the largest proportion of the market possible. If you're looking for units in areas where there is a high percentage of families, you may end up with empty units. Not a good idea. Minimise your risk by ensuring your property matches what the majority require in a property. For instance, if the suburb has a high proportion of single people, don't buy a one-bedroom unit as only single people, first home buyers or couples can live there. Buy a two-bedroom unit so you also get the additional market of the young family, the shared accommodation and maybe even downgraders (that is, retiring baby boomers).

So, getting to know the people who live in the suburbs you're considering will help you narrow down your search, sometimes right down to the street you want to buy on.

Toolbox tip

Sign up for Google alerts for your suburbs and towns. As soon as there is mention of your area, for instance that a new highway to bypass this town is being built or new train line to connect this suburb is planned, you can be on top of drivers of population and capital growth. Highway bypasses have killed off many small towns throughout Australia.

The best way to make solid investment decisions is to get to know the suburbs or towns you've selected. We're really narrowing things down. Targeting areas that are likely to soon suffer economic downturns is not a good decision, but neither is following the crowd and purchasing in an area just because everyone else is. Make sure that the suburbs you're considering are going to grow in population, in demand, economically, and so on. Do the research. This leads us to every property investor's best friend: the internet.

Toolbox tip

Be sure to vary your property locations as your portfolio increases. This will give you exposure to different stages of the market. For example, as Perth goes up in value, the Sydney market may be decreasing in value, so you may be able to access equity from the Perth property to grow your portfolio. But remember to be aware of your properties being cross-collateralised as this can prevent you from being able to access any capital gain. If you are cross-collateralised, lenders will look at your entire asset value, so if your Sydney property has a lower value and your Perth property a higher value, the overall value may not have changed and the lender sees no new equity for you to access. However, if the properties are viewed separately you could access the equity from the Perth property without the value of the Sydney property ever being an issue. (We covered this in chapter 9.)

You will be able to find 80 per cent of what you want to know about a suburb on the internet and you don't have to pay a fortune for it either. Over the past 10 years, I have collated more than 30 websites that I use to gather information and assess an area. This enables me to drill down and find a specific property. All of these sites are free.

Toolbox tip

When searching on a real estate sales site, enter a price range 10 to 20 per cent above and below your median price as you may be able to negotiate down or there may be some already heavily reduced properties

Toolbox tip (*cont'd*)

that meet your criteria. Hence, if your median is $300000, search for properties priced between $240000 and $360000. If you have decided on a renovation-and-sell strategy, you may have to buy closer to the $200000 price mark (when you back-calculate your numbers) to make a decent return. (Check out part III of the book if this is what you are planning to do.)

There are so many new and emerging websites with great, often free, data. Visit <www.yourpropertysuccessnow.com.au/ypsbookbonus> for an updated listing.

CHAPTER 12

Hitting the streets

Finally it's time to hit the streets and pound the pavement. It's time to actually visit some of the properties you've selected. Make sure you have a good list of properties in your selected suburbs and map out your route.

Many real estate experts insist that you need to see 100 properties in order to weed out what you don't want and target what you do want. If you look at 100 properties and end up with one that fits your criteria, don't fret; you're doing well! Remember, you want to make wise choices and good buys. Keep your buying criteria close at hand and don't succumb to an emotional purchase.

In 2002 Todd and I looked at 178 properties in three months. We put offers in on 12, had five offers accepted and bought two. So I agree with the 'see one hundred, buy one property' adage. Remember: it is hard work.

You should be using checklists to gather information about the properties you visit. Don't leave the particulars to memory! Write everything down and take photos!

Your property inspection checklist

What you include in your inspection checklist is important. Begin with the basics: address, date of visit, age of property, and so on. Then you need to make note of the property's most distinctive features. This is important, because if you notice something (good or bad), a potential buyer or renter is likely to notice the same thing. What stands out about the property? Does it have a distinctive design? Is it between two dilapidated buildings? This information will not only help you remember the property, it will help you gauge the profitability of the property. For instance, a distinctive design may help the property sell faster. Being sandwiched between two distressed properties may keep the property from selling altogether.

Ask why the owners are selling. This can also be important to know, and can give you information you don't already have. If the homeowner is selling because the neighbourhood isn't what it used to be, you might want to think twice about buying the property.

Visit <www.yourpropertysuccessnow.com.au/ypsbookbonus> and download a checklist.

The inspection

Take your time and walk through each property. Using your checklist, make note of the rooms each property has and the specific features of each room. Make note of needed or desired repairs and renovations and give the property an overall ranking for appearance. List everything that might affect you. For example, an older house with one power point in the bedroom might require a second power point. After pulling off skirting boards, paying the electrician's time, repainting and plastering, you may be lucky if it only costs you $500. You need to be thinking about, or know this, ahead of time.

Toolbox tip

Add to your list of properties a few that are at the upper end of the median price range if you are considering renovating. Go and have a look at the finished product. Take notes about the features and changes you may want to make during your renovation. I have done this many times and found that my grand renovation plans were actually too much for the market and I could tone them down and save money. You seriously have to consider whether a Caesarstone benchtop is appropriate for an area or whether it's just over the top. This small exercise will help you make those decisions.

Now check out the neighbourhood features. You may need to drive around to do this. Are the roads in good shape? What is the condition of the surrounding properties? How close is the property to schools, shopping centres and transportation?

The more information you record, the better your analysis of the property. You'll learn as you go along what's important and what's not. But, for now, it's best to err on the side of caution and have too much information rather than not enough.

Take your time at each property; you don't want to miss anything and have to come back. Yes, it can take you only five minutes to assess a property—make those minutes count. It's not possible to remember everything, so take photos, staple the brochure to your checklist and move on to the next one. This is another reason it's a good idea to select suburbs close to each other; you'll not only have a more consistent demographic, but you can fit more inspections into one day.

Toolbox tip

Keep a few bananas and Red Bulls in the car. Someone is going to get stressed (usually the driver) and a sugar hit will be needed.

When you finish your inspections, go over each checklist and rank each property on a scale of 1 to 10. You can put each property on an even scale by giving each one an overall ranking. Then sort your properties by ranking, with 10 being the best properties and 1 being the worst.

Remember the low-risk approach: hold tightly onto your checklist, and just to be safe, take your buying criteria with you as well. Complete each checklist religiously and remember to rank the properties. Don't let your emotions guide your choices. Facts only!

Toolbox tip

Here's a secret: you may not believe it now, but once you are so focused on what you want and where you want it, you'll find a deal of a lifetime every week because you'll know what you're looking for. Seriously. With this knowledge you are 99 per cent ahead of others in the market, which might not make you immune to losing out on properties (because some people will pay more than the property is worth), but when you do get your property it will be one that will get you to your goals.

I can guarantee, after a few weeks, 90 per cent of your choices will be weeded out before you even inspect and you will know within five minutes at the inspection if the property is for you. Within two months and with 100 inspections under your belt, you will be able to spot a bargain a mile away.

Check your list

It may seem anticlimactic but, now that you've visited what seems like about a trillion properties, you'll want to go back home (or to your office) and sift through all your checklists.

If you've followed the plan, you now have a ton of information. You will need to sort through all of this information before you forget any specifics you may have missed during your home inspections.

If you think back to the fundamentals, there were three things on which you based your pre-inspection decisions:

$ *Your property investment strategy.* Does the property fit with my strategy? If not, toss it.

$ *Your buying criteria.* Have they all been met? If not, toss it or reassess what you are willing to compromise on.

$ *What you can afford.* There's no use in finding the perfect property and then not to being able to afford it. If you're planning on renovating and it's going to cost you $60 000, not $20 000, because of the state of the property, then know that now.

The good, the bad and the ugly

Okay. So now you're sitting at a table; you have thrown out the properties that did not match the three points above; and you're still completely surrounded by stacks of checklists and piles of notes. But don't stress — this isn't going to be as hard as it looks if you follow these steps.

Step 1

Gather your data for each suburb and each property. Double check that the properties fit what you expect for the area; for example, that the median is a two-bedroom house with a garage.

Step 2
Check the expected sale price for the properties; if there are any that are way over your budget, don't waste any more time on them. Keep an eye on them in case there are any dramatic changes. Don't actually throw the checklists away. File them somewhere. They may come in handy in the future. Make note on the checklist why the property has been excluded.

Step 3
You should now have a group of properties that represent your strategy, criteria and budget. Make sure that the pile of properties is sorted into ranking order, from 10 to one.

Toolbox tip

Remember to continue to monitor all the properties you have visited. You can find sale results in the weekend newspapers or from the real estate agent.

Are you done? Well, yes, for now you are done. You've accomplished everything we set out to do in this chapter. You have selected potential properties that suit your own personal real estate investment goals.

Now that you have completed your property visits, and you have matched properties to your strategy and your criteria, you have a group of potential properties that have been thoroughly researched and fit your goals as an investor. Ideally, you've made it through the elimination process with no emotion. Don't save a property because 'it might pan out' or 'it looks good' or 'a friend said it was a good deal'. Base each elimination, or selection, on the solid strategies and criteria that we've worked hard to develop. After all, your goal is to make money, right? You should now know the areas so intimately that you can identify opportunities to buy below the market, like we discussed earlier with one of the prongs of the Trident Strategy (see figure 6.1 on p. 44). Your buying criteria would have included your requirements for future capital growth—another of the three prongs of the Trident Strategy.

Now you have a great bunch of properties that fit your personal investment goals so you're ready to make an offer. In chapter 13 we'll delve deep into the remaining prong of the Trident Strategy—renovation.

CHAPTER 13

Finding a renovator's dream

In chapter 10 we looked at locating your property. We started with thousands of suburbs and towns and worked our way down to three. For some readers your property investing strategy has been achieved and you are ready to purchase. For those of you who added renovation to your strategy, this section is for you. We need to take this further and look at assessing the area you have chosen for renovation potential. Remember the Trident Strategy prongs—adding value and creating equity in the medium term.

You need to look at streets within your suburb with an eye for renovation potential. If you were doing structural renovations you would be trolling council websites looking for their heritage overlay plans, zoning and any relevant restrictions on how much of the property can be taken up with buildings. From a cosmetic point of view you can also go a degree further in your research and look at which streets will deliver you more value.

Later on we will cover how you can develop your own rule of thumb about the price you should pay for a property. There is a differential between renovated and unrenovated properties. This may be around 30 to 35 per cent depending on the profit you want. So you need to know where this variation is.

Now that you have chosen suburbs that are forecasting good capital growth with median property values in your buying range it's time to look for properties listed for sale in streets with the highest price distribution ranges. This is because there's little point in spending money on any renovations that go beyond a simple makeover in streets where every property has the same appearance and value.

CEO and founder of Residex John Edwards believes that the worth of the best property in a street sets a benchmark against which the prices of all other properties in the street will be measured. He says, 'If there is little price difference between the best property in the street and the worst, your opportunities to achieve uplift in value are severely limited.'

Choosing properties

Having researched on the ground and selected some suitable streets, the next step is to look for listings at the low end of each street's price range. Whether you are proposing to undertake a quick renovation (which we will look at later) or more extensive renovations, your aim is to lift the renting or selling power of your property compared to the others in the street.

I have found the *Renovator's Report* produced by Residex a useful tool that quickly enables me to see the street by street price differential. The greater the range of prices, the higher the potential value you can add to your property after you have completed the renovation. For more information on how to use this report, visit <www.yourpropertysuccessnow.com.au/ypsbookbonus>.

Once you have narrowed your search down to the street level where you should be targeting, you need to start looking at properties to assess what can be done, how much value you can add and how much it will all cost.

This is a good place to do a quick double check on what the median property looks like and comparing it against your buying criteria. You need to know who you are targeting as the renter or buyer. If the price range is at the premium end of the market (for instance, over $800 000), you need to consider that people want everything—alarms, ducted vacuum systems, and so on. These things don't come cheap (an alarm system can cost $2000). For a $350 000 property you would not go overboard on these things.

Renovation strategies

Experts say the wisest idea is to only make improvements that will add to the resale value of your property. Indeed, the aim of renovating as a strategy is to increase the value of your property by substantially more than what you are going to spend on the renovations.

During a boom, people could buy a property within 15 kilometres of the CBD and sit back and get annual growth of between 10 and 20 per cent.

The value went up so quickly that you could refinance and renovate, and the capital growth would pay for the renovation. You could do some renovation and safely assume that, thanks to soaring property values, by the time you'd finished and perhaps enjoyed the property for a few years, you could have paid for the renovation and made some money.

'There is no doubt that when the market is performing well, it may only take a short time — about two years — to recoup what you've spent,' says Jim Brennan, a property valuer with Sydney-based Herron Todd White. 'But it can take a lot longer when the market is flat,' he says.

I am going to touch on this briefly. My property investing strategies are about low risk and arguably you could read this as low return. However, because I use my Trident Strategy I am actually making money on three fronts to increase the return. My strategy is about building a portfolio for the long term and for sustainable wealth. Many investors want or need money now to do other things and increase their immediate available net worth as opposed to their net worth being locked away as equity in a property. Renovation can be used as a strategy to do this as well.

Flipping is the term given to buying and selling within a short period of time — usually including a renovation. This involves buying well, renovating and selling, preferably in the same market. There are great benefits to doing this. Essentially, your bank account goes up quickly if you do it correctly. Getting it wrong is where the risk lies. The biggest risk is that you cannot recover your costs: buying costs — including the hefty stamp duty cost — selling costs, holding costs and the renovation costs. Your renovation profit has to cover all costs before you see any dollars in your pocket. Also remember that in Australia if you sell within 12 months you will be up for capital gains tax on 100 per cent of the gain you have made. If you sell after 12 months of the purchase date you only pay tax on 50 per cent of the gain (this differs from state to state). So to maximise your return you would need to go through the process of getting tenants and making sure that the area has good underpinning capital growth fundamentals, that is, demand. So all three prongs of the Trident low-risk investment strategy would have to be at work here.

Many a clever investor has seen the opportunity to live in a property, renovate and sell without paying capital gains. Although in theory this is a clever strategy, the ATO is onto this one. They don't actually say how many homes in how many years you can flip before they start considering you an investor, but they are watching. So you may be able to pull this off once or twice but be aware.

Trading properties is also fraught with risk in a market that is changing. I have had clients who bought a property with the flipping strategy in mind and six months later when they are finished and ready to sell the market has dropped and gobbled up all their profits. As long as you have plan B (being able to afford to hold the property) in mind — as you should with any strategy — it is only a delay in executing your plan, and one that will get you some capital gains tax savings.

Many first-time investors look at this strategy as an easy way to make money quickly so they can afford a buy and hold strategy. At the renovation for prosperity seminars I hold throughout Australia there are always a few people in each class who plan on giving up their job and renovating. It sounds easy and they don't realise until they start how much hard work is involved and that the glorified television renovation shows they watch are not true to reality. And those who have not done it before and perhaps do understand the hard work involved are not prepared for the basics. The fact is if you don't have a job the banks won't lend you money. So don't give up your job — yet. You need it to get going and to be able to afford to keep going.

Flipping

Okay, here are the facts. From what I have seen, most flips flop, mainly because the people doing them don't understand the numbers. Here is an example of the costs you would expect from a flip.

Example

Let's say you're buying in an area with a median price of $550 000. We'll work through what you need to buy the property *and* make money.

End value post renovation: $550 000

Acquisition costs: $15 000

Holding costs for six-month renovation: $16 500 (assuming you have used equity to buy the property and interest rates are 7.5 per cent)

Renovation cost: $40 000

Profit margin $40 000 (so for every dollar you spend you make another dollar)

So, to make a profit before tax of $40 000 you have to buy the property at approximately $440 000.

To sum up: you buy a property for less than $440 000. You renovate it with a budget of $40 000 up to a value of $550 000. This may sound like a big ask, and it is. This is why many flips actually flop, because people don't allow for all the costs. Even selling costs can be 2 per cent of your selling price. This is why you need to find the right property, below market value with no significant issues to make this work. Take into account that with a budget of $40 000 this will not be a high value add structural renovation this would be more in the ballpark of a rejuvenate type renovation (see list of renovation types on pp. 152–155). That's why you need to be in the market all the time: so you can jump on these opportunities. You will often find that the property that you end up buying will be advertised at a higher price, and you may be able to negotiate it down to the price you need it to be in order to make a profit. You need to know your numbers and be able to identify opportunities. On a personal note, I haven't undertaken the flipping strategy, but I have worked with people who have been successful with a flip.

The hidden costs
The flipping strategy is based on reselling the property quickly. This means that you will probably sell within 12 months of exchanging contracts and you will pay tax on 100 per cent of the capital gain.

A capital gain (or capital loss) is the difference between what it cost you to acquire an asset and what you received when you disposed of it, according to the ATO. You pay tax on any capital gain. It's not a separate tax, just part of your income tax, although it is generally referred to as capital gains tax (CGT).

You will find that most people who teach the flipping strategy gloss over the capital gain and leave that out of the costings. Often this is because they suggest you can work your way around this if you have a fancy trust structure for ownership, which enables you to legally minimise your tax. This is an expensive option, so let's assume that an average person is just going to buy this property in their own name and not employ any fancy ownership structures.

For the following example we will assume that you earn $79 000 from a normal PAYG job and you resell your property within 12 months. Table 13.1 (overleaf) lists the figures.

Table 13.1: example of costs associated with a flip

Sale proceeds		$550 000
Cost base		
Purchase price	$440 000	
Purchase costs	$15 000	
Holding costs	$16 500	
Renovation costs	$40 000	
Selling costs (2%)	$11 000	
Total cost base		$522 500
Gross capital gain		$27 500
Tax (before capital gain)		
Income from other sources		$79 000
Tax at 30% tax rate		$17 250
Medicare levy (1.5%)		$1 185
Total tax		$18 435
Tax (after capital gain)		
Income from other sources		$79 000
Add gross capital gain		$27 500
Total taxable income		$106 500
Tax at 37% tax rate		$27 355
Medicare levy (1.5%)		$1 598
Total tax		$28 935
Difference in tax due to capital gain*		**$10 518**

Note: *calculation is based on the assumption that there are no capital losses.

Using this strategy, your total costs are $533 018 (including the purchase). You sell for $550 000 and your profit is $16 982. Not a lot of profit for six months' work, is it? Or is it? If you did two of these a year, would that be enough of an income for your contribution to the family finances? Perhaps it would be if you could cut your costs and increase your profit. But be aware that you are increasing your capital gain. For example, if you bought the property for $400 000 and all the assumptions were the same as in table 13.1, your additional tax would be $25 917 with a profit of $41 583. Visit <www.yourpropertysuccessnow.com.au/ypsbookbonus> to see the spreadsheet.

Think about this for a moment: if you set your renovation cost at $40 000, you need to buy at approximately $400 000, complete the renovation and arrive at an end value of $550 000. That's a tall order. With this strategy, all too often the selling costs and capital gains tax are neglected in the initial numbers. You can't afford to ignore these costs.

That's not to say that I don't think the flipping strategy is a good one, especially if you want to build up your cash base using other people's money to make you money. Just be aware that you may be trading one job for another that delivers no certain payout figure.

I do see great opportunity in finding a very large one-bedroom or two-bedroom older style apartment, completing a quick, six-week renovation and then selling for a profit. A deal I assessed in 2011 involved a $400 000 one-bedroom unit that could be reconfigured with a renovation budget of $60 000. It involved moving the kitchen to the front of the unit where the view was looking over Sydney Harbour and creating two bedrooms out of the existing kitchen as well as a very large lounge room. The end valuation on such a unit would be $650 000. So you see it is possible to deliver an $80 000 profit based on the income assumption we used above. I suggest, however, that you refine your renovation techniques before you consider flipping. Have the equity and experience behind you and make sure you have plan B as a backup as well.

Financing a flip

Remember that lenders are in the business of making money. Although exit fees are now a thing of the past and it may seem easy to get finance, do a renovation and then sell, you should remember that each time you fill out a credit application you are adding to your credit profile and lenders may begin to consider you as a risk based on having a number of credit applications in one year. Lenders want long-term clients who will stay with the bank and who have more than two products with them; for example, a loan, credit card and savings account.

After a flip or two you may find that you only have a limited number of lenders willing to lend to you. The more experienced property investors have a large line of credit against existing properties. They tap into the equity in the properties they already own to purchase and renovate a new property without ever actually getting a loan against the property they are buying. This does not affect their credit file.

Now let's compare flipping with the more conservative renovation strategy of buy, renovate and hold.

Toolbox tip

If you are buying without a loan against the property (for instance, you may have enough equity from another property), use this as a negotiation tool. In other words, 'I have the funds now. You don't have to wait for valuations and lender's approval so we don't need a cooling-off period. Here is the cash. By the way, I am only going to offer $400 000. Do you want to do the deal?' So if you ask all the right questions and the agent tells you that the owner needs to sell and you have the cash, this is an opportunity that could get you the property not only below market value but also at a price to make a flip profitable.

Buy, renovate and hold

The alternative to a flip is the buy, renovate and hold strategy. Okay, so it sounds boring compared to the fast in-and-out flip strategy but it can be a tried and true way to build wealth. The thing most people don't realise is that you don't have to sell to get control of the new equity you have created from your renovation. You can simply ask your lender for some of the equity you created.

The initial loan you take out against a property, be it your home or as an investment, is the maximum loan on which you can tax deduct interest for that property. So, if you want to access equity from your investment property to purchase another investment property, the interest on the new loan—although secured against your first investment property—is always attributed to the second property. There are some clever ways of maximising the initial loan amount; however, that is advanced information, which we will not be able to cover here. Nevertheless, the good thing about how the ATO attributes the loan interest is that the equity you take out of your home for the purpose of buying an investment property always makes the interest on that loan tax deductible, even though the loan is secured against your home. How cool is that? A tax-deductible loan against your home. The key is paying down your home loan—that is, the non-deductible debt—first and then moving on to the deductible debt.

Let's assume you bought an investment property with an 80 per cent loan. To fund the 20 per cent deposit and associated purchase costs you use funds from your home or another investment property. These costs are usually accessed through a line of credit secured against your home. Figure 13.1 shows how you may be able to access these funds (we looked at this in depth in chapter 8).

Figure 13.1: accessing equity from one property to purchase another property

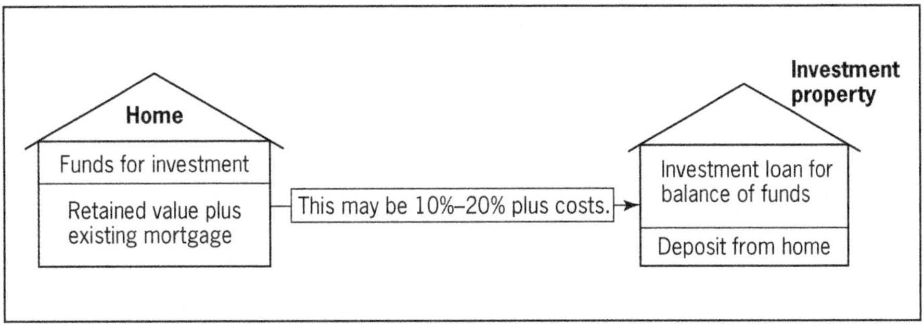

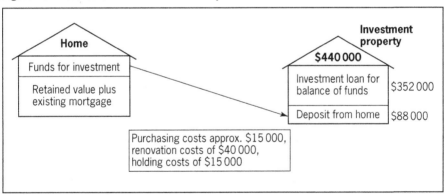

So you can see how to get funds from your home to purchase your first investment property (or the next one!). Figure 13.2 uses the example we looked at earlier, where you bought a property for $440 000 and you renovated it up to $550 000. Note that the funds needed for the renovation, the deposit, the purchasing costs and the holding costs come from the new loan against your home.

Figure 13.2: source of funds for investment purchase

So if you don't flip and sell and make $16 982, what's the alternative? How do you get your hands on the money to repeat the process? You just repeat the process shown in figure 13.2 to access funds from the first investment property to buy the second investment property, as you can see in figure 13.3 (overleaf).

Let's assume you want to retain a loan-to-value ratio of 80 per cent on your first investment property, which is now worth $550 000.

$$\$550\,000 \times 0.8 = \$440\,000$$

Figure 13.3: using equity to build your portfolio

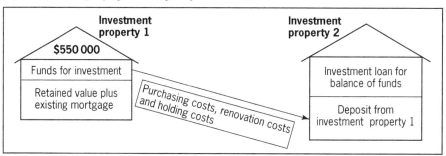

This is how much you have available if you leave 20 per cent of the property value in the property. However, remember that you also have the original loan of $352 000 so you only have new equity of $88 000 ($440 000−$352 000).

This $88 000 is the funds you can use for the next investment property. Or if you are well down the path of investment it could go into a revamp strategy as we discussed above. You could even use the funds for personal use (but then the interest on that loan would not be deductible).

Comparing the two strategies

When flipping, you take the deposit and costs from the equity in your home. So, using the example above, you would take out $88 000 for the deposit and $70 000 for the purchasing, renovating and holding costs (a total of $158 000). You sell the property and repay $352 000 to the lender, $9858 in capital gains tax and $11 000 in selling costs, leaving you with your profit which you could put back into the line of credit (LOC) loan. And your line of credit against your home is replenished. You now have not $158 000, as you did before, but $175 642 (your $17 642 profit) to go and do it all again. Incrementally, your profit becomes higher and you can use that to pull funds for your next purchase.

With the buy, renovate and hold strategy, your initial LOC is not replenished as you are keeping the property so you need to pay interest on that. However, you now have $88 000 to go towards acquiring a second property.

Remember that you needed $158 000 to pull off the first purchase so you will be short if you do the same again with an 80 per cent lend. Thus you could buy a cheaper property or you could go for a 10 per cent deposit ($115 000) and use savings to make your second property purchase. There are a number of ways you can move towards the second purchase.

This is where your initial financial strategy comes into play. If you did have $158 000 available in funds from your home initially and you paid mortgage insurance and only contributed a 10 per cent deposit initially or when you refinanced your investment property — that is, you refinanced to a 90 per cent LVR — you would have additional funds to buy a second property of the same value sooner. Confusing isn't it? What you need to know is that you only get one chance to set yourself up correctly (unless you sell and start again), so get someone such as an experienced mortgage broker or a loan manager on board to help with your big-picture goals.

The key with the flipping strategy is that you cash out and make your money. In the buy, renovate and hold strategy you access equity *and* you get the property growing in value. If you look at the high capital growth prong on the Trident Strategy, you would buy in an area that is outperforming the median (let's say growth is 7 per cent per annum). Using our previous example, $550 000 × 0.07 means that in the first year the value of the property would go up by $38 500 (that is, your property is now worth $588 500). If you were following the flipping strategy when you sold the property you would lose access to those funds for ever (that is, you don't get access to the growth of the property as you don't own it).

The flipping strategy is fraught with danger for the newbie. It is dependent on the time it takes to do the renovation, your tight control of costs and the market cycle you are in. Obviously, if you are in a falling market then the initial property value and median values are reducing as well. Renovation flip stories are similar to those of fishermen or gamblers: you only hear about the wins. In reality successful flips are few and far between unless you are really experienced or go in with your eyes wide open to the numbers involved.

Regardless of how you plan to exit your renovation you need to actually know how to be precise with your renovation costs and work out whether there is a deal to be done or not. After all, anyone can renovate. It's making money out of the renovation that you want to concentrate on.

Assessing potential renovation properties

Although everything may look fine on paper, on further investigation there may be no potential to renovate a property, or the cost to bring the property to the median price for the area is just too high. You need to see where you can create value and what you should be looking for at inspections.

With any renovation project there are points you need to consider when looking at a property. You don't get to the point of signing a contract for a property that you are preparing to renovate without already knowing the following:

$ What needs to be done? (Assess a property for renovation potential.)

$ How much will it cost?

$ Will it deliver value?

If the property passes these hurdles, you need to look closer and ask the following questions:

$ How long will it take?

$ What will the holding costs be?

$ What will the property be worth afterwards?

$ How much of a buffer will I need for the unexpected?

 Toolbox tip

If renovation is your strategy then look for property advertisements that indicate this. These might include 'Renovation Delight', 'Original Features' and 'Charming'. The real estate agent understands that their job is to appeal to the largest market available so they often do a bit of the work for you and identify some of the opportunities an investor would find attractive.

We have already looked at a number of renovation strategies. As I mentioned, the most affordable, quickest and easiest are cosmetic renovations so that is what I am going to concentrate on. There are different types of cosmetic renovations: refresh, repair and rejuvenate.

What you want to know is where you can spend the least amount of money to add the most value as quickly as possible. The answer is often right in front of you: you need to know what your target demographic is after. So once you have selected your three or so areas, start visiting open homes priced at about ten per cent above the median for the area. Check out the finishes and what is typical, and start making a list. This could include the finishes detailed in table 13.2, depending on the area.

Table 13.2: levels of finishes based on price

Low price range <$250 000	Median price range $250 000–$500 000	Higher price range $500 000–$800 000
No dishwasher	White dishwasher	Stainless steel appliances
Bars on windows	Fans in some rooms	Reverse cycle ducted air-conditioning
Carport	Single garage	two-car garage
Laminex benchtops	Laminex benchtops	Caesarstone benchtops
Shower and toilet in the same room	Shower, bath and toilet in same room	Separate toilet and ensuite

You will notice in table 13.2 that I have capped the higher price range at $800 000. Above this price you are entering into the owner-occupier space and the high-end renter space, which is an entirely different category that should be assessed separately. These price ranges also vary by location, so create your own low, median and high ranges.

Once you have created this list you need to go and visit rental open homes on at least one for every 10 'for sale' properties you visit. See what potential tenants are looking for, discussing with the agent how much properties are renting for and how quickly they rent. Get to know the rental market really well as this is where your property will end up.

Toolbox tip

While inspecting rental properties, check out the person showing the property. This will potentially be the person showing yours. You should be looking for a proactive professional rental manager who points out features, not the junior person from the office who one day hopes to become a real estate agent and who spends more time on Facebook than talking face to face to potential tenants

Once you have your list of finishes people want in your area, you can start looking at properties (below the median) that will enable you to add those features and get rewarded for it. In part III we will look at how to work out the purchase price bracket you should consider looking at.

Assuming you are going to take on the rejuvenation type of cosmetic renovation, what should you be looking for? This is when you need a checklist.

Create the checklist of features that are required in your potential property. Print out lots of copies and hit the streets. You should be looking first and foremost for issues — anything that is going to cost you money — and then look at properties that are missing the features that you know would be needed, in other words, create value from nothing.

Visit <www.yourpropertysuccessnow.com.au/ypsbookbonus> to access your 'renovation potential' checklist.

Concentrate on the negative, recognise the positive

You need to start your inspections with the problems that will cost you money and deliver no perceivable value. What you want is bang for your buck. Every dollar you spend needs to make you money — and soon. So if you are spending your $20 000 budget fixing the roof, restumping and repairing termite damage on your property it will possibly not go up in value at all — not even by the money you have spent.

Essentially, you are only at the starting point. If there is nothing obvious wrong with the property and you have progressed to the point of submitting an offer then you should get a builder — not necessarily your building inspector — to visit the property, do a thorough investigation and tell you what they consider are the issues and associated costs. Generally your building inspector will not provide this information unless you request it.

Thus, for everything you note down that includes spending dollars, ask yourself: will this add value? Or, can I negotiate at least the cost to repair this problem off the price?

Plan where you spend your money

Obviously, the refresh strategy is the cheapest and quickest one. Good looking properties will naturally be attractive to live in, so it makes sense to start with the basics of cleaning windows, removing clutter from around the property, mowing lawns and trimming edges, removing unappealing and overgrown plant areas, getting the carpet professionally cleaned and removing unsightly window coverings. These basic upgrades can be done for a few thousand rather than tens of thousands of dollars and often can be the starting point for home improvements.

The repair strategy may include painting both inside and outside, sanding the floor, updating the light switches and power points, new door handles, a new benchtop on top of an existing kitchen, resurfacing the bath and even painting over tiles to give the kitchen and the bathroom a lift.

The rejuvenation strategy targets the two biggest potential money-making areas: the kitchen and the bathroom. These are usually complete refits. Make sure you make them to a consistent standard for what the market wants — or a little bit better, so you rent faster.

In addition to these areas you should be looking at making the place light, bright and liveable. This might mean adding skylights. It will definitely involve repainting the property. By far, these are the areas where you're going to be getting more value than the dollars you spend.

In chapter 18 I will examine each of the areas and look at what you might do to add value and what to be aware of. I will also share some of my tips and renovating mistakes for each one. Take these tips and suggestions and keep them in mind when you are inspecting a property. You could even add them to your checklist. When you go through a property I suggest that you tag each room and major components in the room with the following words (you can even add them to your checklist):

$ *Retain*. This is an existing feature that you do not need to touch.

$ *Remove*. This is looking at things that just have to go.

$ *Renovate*. This is looking for features that you can improve on.

With these in mind, assess each room for what you need to fix, bin or improve. Remember, you are going to be looking at these properties quickly and you will usually spend less than 10 minutes in each one, so having a checklist that you can tick and flick so you don't forget anything is crucial. Simply staple the property flyer the agent gives you (or one you download from the internet) to the checklist and you can quickly review properties.

Toolbox tip

Keep your property inspection notes. On your inspection checklist from chapter 12 you might note down things that you could do to add value.

Next we will look at how you go about purchasing your investment property.

CHAPTER 14
Purchasing your property

It is said that 'the devil is in the detail'. No truer words could be spoken for the property buyer. You have already:

$ assessed your goals

$ studied the various investment strategies

$ decided on your own path and established your buying criteria; that is, your checklist for purchasing a property.

These three things form the foundation of a long-term, successful property investment portfolio.

Next you assessed your funds and how much the property would cost you. Then came the 'fun' part: digging for the diamond; that is, locating the property that will be perfect for your needs.

The job does not stop here. In fact, the period between you deciding to put in an offer on the property and the actual settlement, which is usually about six weeks later, is just as crucial.

There is a range of issues to deal with from when you sign the contract of sale through to actually settling on the property and picking up the keys. Here are some points to note.

$ What do you need to include in your letter of offer?

$ Have you considered all your negotiating options?

$ Have you organised a building inspection?

$ Are there tax benefits to be gained in the purchase and if so what are the steps to activating these?

$ Are you considering a quick renovation? If so don't wait until you get the keys — start working on it now!

$ How will you screen tenants?

$ Who is going to arrange your property inspection?

$ Is your property adequately protected?

$ Do you have a conveyancer or solicitor who can act quickly and let you know of any issues?

Properties can be sold in any of three ways: they may go to auction, be advertised on the market or go to tender. The latter is usually reserved for very expensive properties, so let's leave that one for now.

Although auctions are a popular spectator sport according to Australian Property Monitors (January 2012), fewer than 13 per cent of properties are sold at auction, so we will concentrate on private sales. Note that it is possible to make an offer before an auction, so the information below is just as relevant to properties being auctioned.

Questions to ask the agent

Remember that the real estate agent is working for the vendor. They are often privy to the vendor's motivations for selling, asking price, bottom line and much more. Your job is to find out as much as you can. Start with these questions:

$ Is the vendor interested in offers?

$ How motivated is the vendor (is it a family breakup, are they under financial stress or are they downsizing?)

$ Have you had any other offers?

$ What were the offers?

You should also be asking the obvious questions:

$ Is the property rented?

$ How long is the lease?

$ What is the weekly rent?

Toolbox tip

If the tenants have decided not to be pushed around and inconvenienced by property inspections, they may decide to stay put during the inspection. Use them as a resource and ask them about the property.

Why is the vendor selling? This is a great question that rarely gets answered but if you find out the vendor has bought elsewhere or is moving overseas or the property is part of a deceased estate there will usually be some urgency and negotiation opportunities. So always ask — just in case.

As you have chosen your three suburbs and you know that you have at least 100 physical inspections ahead of you, it is likely that you are going to start running into the same agents a few times, so get to know them and find who in the agency is listing the properties you're interested in. These people can become your greatest allies.

Picture this. An agent meets a potential vendor. They know this property fits your criteria because you have told them what they are. (You may need to 'educate' them about how to spot a property that meets your needs.) They call you and say that the property will be on the market in a few weeks. If they can do the deal prior to having to hold open homes and don't have to go through expensive marketing campaigns everyone is happy. In a rising market where there is not a lot of room for negotiation and the vendor knows the going sale prices — and you are seeing rapidly increasing sale prices — buying now at their asking price could be a great decision.

I always apply my pink panther spy position at open homes. This just means I try to overhear all the conversations the agent is having. It's amazing what you can learn.

This is how buyer's agents work. They know the real estate agents so well that as soon as a property is on the agent's books they call buyers who might be interested. So nurture your relationships with the real estate agents in your area as you want them calling you with any opportunities.

Another way to make sure they keep you up to date on other offers is to ask for a copy of the contract. Depending on which state you are buying in, these can usually be emailed to you immediately.

Buying below the market

As one of the prongs of the Trident Strategy I suggest you buy below the market. How do you do this and why would a vendor sell below the market price? A vendor might be motivated to sell below the market due to their personal circumstances. You may have heard of the 3 'Ds'.

$ *Death.* Usually the property is sold by the family.

$ *Divorce.* The vendors need to sell quickly to exit any jointly held assets.

$ *Debt.* Due to personal circumstances the vendor needs to sell quickly.

Well, I think there are four more 'Ds':

$ *Desperation.* The property has been on the market for awhile or the vendor may have bought elsewhere and need to settle quickly.

$ *Disappointment.* This could be a someone who planned to purchase with the view of developing, splitting, subdividing and so on, and they were not able to get approval or finance to complete this strategy.

$ *Disillusion.* One of those thousands of investors who buy and their property does not deliver.

$ *Disinterest.* This may be someone retiring and selling up, or for instance overseas owners who no longer require the property for their children to live in while at university.

You need to be able to estimate market value and this comes from visiting properties and recording their sale data. You could get a property below market value for the following reasons.

$ A real estate agent may not appreciate the full value of the property.

$ There could be difficult tenants who prevent access for inspections.

$ The property might have issues that scare others off, including termite damage or rising damp issues.

$ If you know the vendor's motivation for selling you could make the offer based on conditions that suit them. This could include extended settlement, or even a shorter settlement, releasing the deposit, allowing the vendor to rent the property until they find a new home, and so on.

You don't know if it is possible to get a property below market value until you try. So make some cheeky offers.

How much should you offer?

This is a difficult question to answer. The answer is: it depends. In fact, one of the more important factors to consider is where we are in the property cycle. You can get reports monthly that will tell you what houses and units are going for in the capital cities, but we know that there are markets within markets, called submarkets. You want to know what your area is doing. Once again it comes down to the numbers.

Toolbox tip

Usually agents will give you a price range to work within. You need to know your agent is familiar with the area and, as you now know how to do all the research necessary to determine what a property is really worth, don't take their word for it.

Some property websites actually track discounting; that is, the percentage difference between the initial listing price and the sale price. Check out <www.domain.com.au> and go to Suburb Reports where you will find 'Days on the market' and the percentage discount that is currently a condition of the market in that suburb. If the discounting is, say, 2 per cent, I would expect it to be a tightly held area; that is, an area where no-one is selling or prices are moving up. That is, vendors are generally getting what they want. The 'Days on the market' can help substantiate that. If the percentage is higher, say 8 per cent, this is indicative of room for negotiation and that vendors are accepting lower prices than their initial expectations.

Toolbox tip

If I saw that the discounting was at 8 per cent I definitely would be starting my offer at 10 to 12 per cent below the asking price and maybe ending up at 8 per cent. Don't start at the asking price or at the percentage discount price. Leave some room for negotiation.

Obviously, your offer is based on your analysis of many properties and what you think the property owner will accept—not necessarily what the property is worth. Remember the Trident Strategy: buy below the market.

Toolbox tip (*cont'd*)

I cannot tell you how many times an agent has told me my offer was rude or insulting or they would not take it to the owner. That's fine. I can tell you that many a rude, insulting offer has been accepted by a vendor. You never know until you try.

By purchasing a report from Residex CMA, RP Data or Australian Property Monitors, you can find out what the owner bought the property for and when. This can assist you in considering what they may accept as an offer. Obviously, someone who bought 12 months ago for $380 000 may not accept anything less than that unless they were in a really difficult situation. Once again, getting your agent to tell you why they are selling really helps.

Be fair with your offer, but remember: if the numbers don't add up, no matter how much time and effort you have put into the negotiation, walk away. A 'bargain of the century' appears weekly when you know what you are looking for. It is a numbers game — play it but just don't get caught up in the game.

Don't be trapped by the 'meet the vendor halfway' line. For example, you have offered $320 000 and they want $340 000. Your next offer is not $330 000, but it may be $323 000. That is, you are giving a little. Let's assume the vendor says no. They want $335 000. Then your next offer is not halfway — $329 000 — but it may be $325 250. Let them know you know your numbers and especially if you have a renovation strategy that you have assessed things and this is the price that will make the deal viable. That way you are showing them that begrudgingly you are offering a bit more. This can backfire if you want the property and there is money to be made and the asking price is fair going back and forth can upset the vendor. (Mind you the agent will usually let you know if this is happening.)

A final word: you should know what the property is worth. You should know what you need to buy it for to make money. As for fancy auction techniques, leave that to those who are bringing their ego to the table. Get in and secure the property so you can get on with making more money, which will get you to your goals faster. For more information on buying at auction visit my website at <www.yourpropertysuccessnow.com.au/ypsbookbonus>.

The offer

Once you have decided on your maximum purchase price, it's time to make a offer. There are some things you need to include in any offer. The most important things are the price, the duration of the offer and the extras. The extras can be long and convoluted or simple and straightforward.

Toolbox tip

There is one extra that is mandatory, in my opinion, and that's the 'subject to finance' clause. The point of this clause is to give the bank's valuer time to get out and value the property and inform you and the lender that in terms of the security (that is, the property) and the price and any risk associated, it is acceptable to them and they will lend you the money. Different lenders assess risk differently.

It is not necessary to write a letter of offer. You can make a formal offer by submitting a completed and signed Contract of Sale of Real Estate, or even verbally. However, if you want to add any conditions, it is best to get them all in writing. It would be advisable to obtain legal advice prior to signing the contract.

When making your offer, you need to keep in mind what you need is the figure which is your walk-away deal breaker. This is the figure that you will not, under any circumstances, go over. Then consider the terms that you would possibly negotiate to get your offer accepted. For example, you might release the deposit to the vendor in return for a lower offer than the asking price, or a longer settlement time. Or you may allow the vendor to stay in the property and rent it until they buy their next property. This is where knowing about the vendor is important.

You may consider making an offer subject to any or all of the following:

$ *Building and pest inspections.* This is an important clause, as you don't want to find out about pest or structural problems after purchasing the house.

$ *Vacant possession.* This may be necessary if you are doing a renovation. However, be aware of the rental agreement and the notification terms for tenants. This differs from state to state (or territory), but if you have to wait 60 days—or whatever the specific time frame is—you need to consider how that will affect your purchase and the plans for the property.

$ *Finance acceptable to you.* Ideally, you will need to have made your arrangement with the bank before making an offer, so you know how much you can borrow and hence how much you can spend. Once you have decided to commit time to hitting the streets and actually inspecting properties, you should also let your mortgage broker or lender know you need to have your pre-approval processed. The condition that lenders usually have in their conditional (or pre-approval) is that the selected property meets the bank's assessment of its value against the offered price. This is their way of checking that you are not paying too much (so that if you should default they don't end up with a property that's worth less than the loan they have against it). Hence they will need to order a valuation. This will take time, so be patient but make sure you have the time.

Remember that the pre-approval usually only lasts for three months so you don't want it too early. You want to have the best lender offer on the day. Lenders change rates and policies regularly and you don't want unnecessary enquiries on your credit file from pre-approvals that have gone nowhere. Timing is important. Get finance arranged so that as soon as you have an offer accepted you can send the contract of sale, your latest payslips and the rental estimate to your mortgage broker or lender to get pre-approval converted to a formal approval within the small window of the cooling-off period, if you have one.

Each of these conditions would be noted in the letter of offer. Remember that other people may also want to buy this property so the more conditions you include the less attractive your offer may be to the vendor. Stick to those conditions that you really want and be prepared to acknowledge what will be a deal breaker and what you will accept. For example, you may like the Grecian urn out the front, or the chandelier, so you could ask for that to be included, but make it clear that you will not walk away if it is not. However, if you require an extended settlement or you need seven days for the valuation, that wouldn't be negotiable.

You can put down a smaller deposit than the amount stipulated in the contract. In some states this is usually 10 per cent; however, most vendors will accept 5 per cent or even a nominal dollar amount such as $500. You must specify your deposit amount in your letter of offer if it is different from what is in the contract. You don't have to pay the deposit until the offer is accepted. This would in most cases take the property off the market. You may decide not to put down a deposit, however you risk getting gazumped. If you do put the money down though, be prepared that should you not go ahead with the purchase you could incur a penalty of 0.25 per cent of the price of the property. This is the case in New South Wales, although each state and territory has its own statutes in this regard.

During the cooling-off period, which is usually five days (although it could be a condition of your offer that it is longer), you will need to organise the pest and building inspections, get formal loan approval from your lender and do anything else that is a condition of the contract. Achieving all of this in five days is usually difficult. The reason for this is that the bank valuer and the building and pest inspectors need to organise access to the property. There can be delays in getting access, especially when the house or unit is rented out (as opposed to being owner-occupied). For this reason it's worth negotiating an extension to the cooling-off period before signing the contract.

Building and pest inspections

A pre-purchase building inspection can save you thousands.

There is no such thing as a perfect house. Professional property inspector Leon Cupit believes that a professional and independent property inspection should be mandatory in each and every real estate transaction, including new homes. Cupit, who operates Independent Property Inspections, believes that only licensed and registered inspectors should be used. He says, 'Every home stands in silence just waiting for a professional, experienced inspector to uncover and reveal its secrets.'

He says that property defects come in all shapes and sizes from minor wear and tear to significant and costly structural defects.

'And a pre-purchase building inspection carried out before you buy a property will arm you with information that is ... worth its weight in gold.'

The inspection report will identify significant building defects or problems and sometimes even provide repair costs for the defects found. When most people think property inspection they think timber decay or termite damage and the like. But that's merely scratching the surface. The condition of the building and how it may impinge on the value can play a crucial role in what is undoubtedly the most important purchase or sale you will ever make.

Even brand new homes hide secrets that are only obvious to the expert eye of an experienced property inspector. Property faults and defects are often not obvious or may be intentionally hidden and remain undisclosed during the marketing period. An experienced inspector knows what to look for. This could even include legal requirements related to such things as electrical switch boards or fire alarms.

Then there are the defects and problems that are readily visible to everyone and appear cosmetic in nature. Consider for example seemingly minor symptoms such as a sticking door or window. This might reveal major structural movement of the foundation of the building when inspected that escape the attention of the average home buyer who would simply note that the door needs a little shaving off the top.

Leon Cupit stresses that all homes, regardless of age or condition, harbour a list of defects. He notes too that learning just how severe these are, and how long the list of defects is, can have a direct bearing on a purchase decision. It can determine whether you accept these and are happy and satisfied with your well-informed decision to purchase, or whether you become overwhelmed, angry and frustrated when the magnitude of unknown or previously undiscovered or undisclosed defects become apparent after settlement. And then it's too late.

 Toolbox tip

Find out whether someone else has had a pest and building report done on a property you're interested in and ask the real estate agent whether they would share it with you for a percentage of the price.

An inspection can also assist you in knowing which maintenance or repair expenses you are likely to have to incur, and the inspection report could be used as a bargaining tool to lower the purchase price of the property.

 Toolbox tip

Often you can get a greatly reduced price on the cost of an inspection if you ask for a verbal rather than a written report. Regardless, you should always accompany the inspector and try to get the agent to wait at the door. This is because the inspector may pick up an issue and indicate that it would be relatively inexpensive to fix. You can then try to negotiate thousands off the price based on the issue—but that won't work if the agent was standing next to you when you spoke to the inspector.

Look for the major faults and don't let the minor faults trouble you too much. For example, poor guttering is much less of a concern than poor foundations. Importantly, concentrate on any issues that an independent adviser raises when it comes to inspections and checks: real estate agents are *not* independent. And don't use an inspector recommended by an agent. Remember that real estate agents work in the *vendors'* interests.

Toolbox tip

It could be worth checking out the body corporate minutes and notes to see if there is any indication of pests and building issues before you decide to commit money to inspections. Be prepared that these inspections could cost up to $500 each.

Allow yourself enough time to get the information you require and make it a priority from the time you sign the letter of offer. It is your responsibility!

The following list of conditions may not be in your letter of offer, but they do have to be taken care of within the time frame specified in the offer. Check with your solicitor about what specific terms you should include in your offer. An offer may read along the lines of: The offer of (amount) expires on (date) and (time) and is subject to the following conditions.

$ A deposit (amount) or 5 per cent is payable after (number of days) of exchange of contract with balance at settlement.

$ The offer is subject to a building inspection acceptable to me within (number of days).

$ The offer is subject pesticide inspection acceptable to me within (number of days).

$ The offer is subject to finance that is acceptable to me within (number of days). (Note: try to negotiate 10 working days to allow for valuer delays and unexpected delays.)

There are many more conditions that can be added to an offer. The key is the 'acceptable to me' clause. Without it, the vendor could, for example, turn around and give you finance at an interest rate of 20 per cent just so they can sell the property, I that is the only condition holding up the sale then they may satisfy that for you. This is an over the top example but the reasoning is true — this is your offer so you need to stay in charge.

As noted earlier, be prepared to give yourself enough time to get all the checks done. This may mean asking for a longer cooling-off period than is in the standard contract.

CHAPTER 15

The buying process

Now it's time to start the buying process — the long and sometimes complex period of transferring ownership of your chosen property.

Conveyancing

The conveyancing process ensures that you as the buyer of the land should get a clear and marketable title to the land. Conveyancing is the transfer of the legal title of property from seller to buyer. It is designed to ensure that the buyer gets all the rights to the land they purchase. Solicitors and conveyancers are accustomed to seeing contracts, so anything that is unusual or stands out should be picked up quickly. You need to know if the Roads Authority, for example, can compulsorily acquire your property, or whether there is a right of way through your property.

Exchange of contracts

Although it is best to have finance in place first, this is not always the case. However, don't sign anything without getting your conveyancer or solicitor to examine the contract. It's a good idea to ask a solicitor to go through the contract because they would need to look for the existence of mortgages and caveats, easements and other legal instruments that create encumbrances on the land and prevent you from getting clear title.

Toolbox tip

You need to know what to do once you have found a property. In terms of preparing financially for the investment it would be prudent to allow about six per cent of the purchase price for set-up costs.

Strata title property

Far from being low risk, strata buildings, or those where units are controlled by a body corporate, present a potential risk for investors seeking to invest in a unit or townhouse. You could in effect be inheriting a bucketload of problems. These may be financial costs or costs associated with noise, unkempt buildings or disputes between neighbours or, even worse, a builder not fixing problems that should be under their warranty insurance.

Obtaining a strata report

If you're buying a unit, apartment, townhouse or the like that has a body corporate, you would be wise to get a strata report. I cannot stress this enough. When buying a property you're not buying just a specific unit but a development that is maintained, controlled and managed by the corporation of owners (body corporate).

Toolbox tip

If you don't know what to look for, ask your solicitor to arrange a professional to do this for you.

You should thoroughly check the strata report. Check whether the entity managing the building is in good financial health and that the building is being maintained properly. It's important that you examine the records and look forensically at the financial factors. Check how many levies you are responsible for as unit owner. Look also at the proportion of the levies that provides for ongoing expenses such as building insurance and building maintenance, and the proportion that goes into reserve for future maintenance (such as painting or replacement of facilities such as lifts and swimming pools, which can suffer from wear and tear).

You should do your own walk around the building and assess anything obvious in terms of defects (for example, peeling paint, rotting timber; rusty drainpipes). You should look in particular at defects that may need attention, such as concrete cancer, mould, termites or infestation, as these are costs that you will need to contribute to in the future if you own a unit in the building.

By obtaining a strata report you can access all of the following information as well:

$ the strata plan

$ the levies that should be paid to the corporation of owners (including the special levies that the corporation levied in the past)

$ the respective unit entitlements of the owners

$ the by-laws that the residents should abide by — these can be particularly important for people considering renovation, especially where the body corporate has vetoed previous renovation

$ insurance policies which are taken out by the corporation of owners

$ any legal proceedings that involve the corporation of the owners

$ an expense list of the corporation of owners

$ the expenditure of past and future projects including any major repair work

$ a list of previous significant repair works

$ complaints list from the owners and any records of disputes between past or current owners.

Your offer is accepted

Congratulations! Your offer has been accepted and you are now on the way to being a property owner possibly in about six weeks' time. After months of physical inspections and months prior to that of research you are probably 'over it' and wanting to take some time out.

In fact these six weeks is when you really need to keep your eye on the ball. You can rest later. You need to consider the following tasks.

$ *Finalising your finance.* Contracts need to be signed and everything has to be prepared in readiness for settlement. (You don't have to attend settlement personally.)

$ *Interviewing rental managers.* Choose a rental manager who will liaise between you and your tenants.

$ *Organising property insurance.* This will be required by your lender, and landlord's insurance.

$ *Obtaining access to the property.* If you're doing a renovation, one of your conditions may have been to gain access prior to settlement, either to do work or to get quotes. You may also be able to gain access in order to start showing your property to potential tenants and minimise your vacancy time. This is a great condition to add to the letter of offer. (Refer to page 141 for more conditions that can be included in your letter of offer).

There is obviously a lot to do during the period between signing the contract and settlement. What you have learned in this chapter will get you streets ahead of most people. You shouldn't be getting a phone call the day before settlement regarding new requirements or issues because this chapter has taught you how to anticipate them.

Settlement

Well, you've made it through and you're nearly at settlement. There are some things you need to know about the week prior to you becoming the owner of the property.

Sometimes the littlest things can make everything fall over. You need to double check that the bank has a copy of the building insurance and make sure they are ready to settle. You need to be ready too. Your solicitor should ask you to organise a bank cheque for your contribution about three days before settlement. Note that this often will be for a higher amount than you expect as they usually add on their fees and there are also disbursements. Disbursements may be your contribution to paying back the previous owner for their payment of rates, water and so on for the period when you are the owner.

All you need to know now is when you can pick up the keys from the real estate agent so you can get on with either renting out the property or renovating. Celebration time!

Many a new owner has turned up to find the Miele dishwasher has been replaced with a Dishlex or the old tenant still in residence and refusing to move. You want to know these things before settlement, so ensure that you do your final inspection as close to settlement as possible.

This is where the long journey for most investors — those who only ever buy one property — often ends. The property has been purchased, the champagne enjoyed and life goes on.

In part III we are going to take a closer look at the final prong of the Trident Strategy: adding equity through renovation.

PART III

Renovating

This is what you've been waiting for: the actual renovation—what to do, how much it will cost, how you do it, how to manage it and how to realise your value. The potential to turn a passive property investment into a valuable part of your portfolio can be realised through careful planning and detailed research. It is, once again, where savvy investors can turbo charge their property performance.

So let's get going.

CHAPTER 16

Renovating for prosperity

We are increasingly becoming the renovation nation. If it's not a show on television about renovation, then it's someone telling you at a barbecue what they have been doing to their home. The majority of properties throughout Australia are older style properties. While most have had some touch-ups there is always opportunity to do more.

It's not just investors who see the benefit of renovation. Home owners are doing more and more renovations as well. There are large costs associated with buying and selling a property. In fact many home owners could spend more than $30 000 in costs alone to buy and sell a $600 000 home. And when you throw in moving costs and the inconvenience factors, this figure is a lot higher. With a bit extra thrown in, the typical home owner could possibly add a bedroom and ensuite to their existing property. More and more home owners are doing just that.

As home owners get more savvy and start thinking like investors, they will see their home as their greatest investment and start making it do more work for them. That is, they will recognise that on average most Australians move every seven to 12 years and hence if their home is a property people want the owner will get a higher price for it. They can then either upgrade or have funds left over to spend. However, here is my prediction: renovations will become even more common given the shrinking pool of new land and the high transaction costs associated with moving house.

As investors we also recognise the benefit of another prong of my Trident Strategy for low-risk property investing: adding equity. Although there are a few ways to add equity—develop, subdivide, rezone, and so on—in this book we are only looking at what is available to the majority of Australians—renovation.

Creating value

Creating value that you can convert into cash or equity can mean the difference between having a few properties and having a lot of properties. Renovation helps you to 'leapfrog'—that is, use one property to buy another. It's one of the best leverage strategies around, especially as you can be expected to contribute as little as 5 per cent of your own money and leverage 95 per cent of the bank's money.

By adding value through a well-considered strategy, you have the potential to apply the equity towards the purchase of another property. And the beauty is that anyone with some training can do it: it's a myth that you need to be handy or have the ability to design. You can call on experts to do all parts of a renovation for profit: what you have to do is plan and be well organised in order to maximise profits. Your objective is to maximise return whether you are holding or selling.

Reno-nation

In 2012 it was estimated that more than six million Australians would be renovating, spending up to $20 billion with the average cost of a major renovation at over $75 0000 (Housing Industry Association (HIA) data). The median value for houses in Australia's capital city regions (October 2011 Residex data) was $517 500. If the average home renovation is $75 000 we can see that the home owner is spending nearly 15 per cent of the value of their property on renovations. So how much should you spend? This really depends on what type of renovation you are going to do.

If renovation is part of your property investing strategy then you would have already decided on the type of renovation that you can afford and that will get you to your goals quickly. Essentially, there are two types of renovation: cosmetic and structural.

However, these can be broken down further. I believe property renovations fall into one of the following categories, which I term the Rs of renovation:

$ *Refresh*. This is typically a clean-up of a dirty, smelly property. It is by far the easiest type of renovation. It is usually not going to cost you a lot but it may only increase the value of the property incrementally. The benefit of this type of renovation is that it definitely will get you an increase in rent.

$ *Repair.* For this type of renovation you will need to invest in a toolbox. You will be repairing and fixing things up. There may be some expenditure—mainly on crack filler, from my experience—and in some cases improvements to items that are already there such as benchtops. This is a really good renovation strategy for building equity without a lot of funds while improving the look and creating a new feel. You may not really get a lot more rent for this type of renovation, but it will usually mean you rent more quickly as tenants like to have a 'newness' to their rental properties without having to necessarily pay for it in higher rent.

$ *Rejuvenate.* This is the typical renovation strategy. It would normally involve a new kitchen, at least a refresh of the bathroom, new carpet or floor sanding, new window coverings and the age-old fix-all paint job. The cost associated with this type of renovation is really based on the outcome you want, but on average it would be 10 per cent of the purchase price. This would keep the renovation standard comparable to the property value; that is, a $20 000 renovation could suit a $200 000 property but not an $800 000 property. The key here is completing the renovation. That makes the property just a little bit better than the median property for the area; that is, enabling you to rent it quickly and if necessary still making it an affordable property to sell. This will require capital outlay and you would expect to at least double that outlay in new equity created if you do the renovation correctly. This will also increase the rental income.

$ *Restructure.* This is a structural renovation and would require council approval in most cases. It may involve restructuring the back of the property to open up the living area and creating the outside living space or even creating extra rooms upstairs. As these types of renovations require council approvals, as soon as I think of them I think of delays. Thus, as part of your research, you want to know how the council in the areas you are targeting assess these types of works and how long the average application takes. Remember that the time that your property is not available for rent is costing you money from loss of rent and not being able to claim the interest costs associated with your loan. This is usually a high investment for a high return and a much larger rent. However, it requires a lot of funds. I would budget for a minimum of $60 000 and expect a return of triple that.

$ *Restructure with a twist.* A really clever twist to the 'restructure' strategy is to restructure without the time-consuming council process. This is my favourite renovating technique. It involves looking at a property — be it an apartment or a house — and creating new rooms within the existing floor plan. (With some councils, you may need to notify them if you are changing things internally so you should check.) This means you can change a two-bedroom property into a three-bedroom property simply with a new wall.

This does involve a bit more work in thinking creatively, as we will see a bit later, but what it means is that you could bump your property up into the next price range. That is, the median price for a two-bedroom property in your area may be $450 000 and a three-bedroom one could be $600 000. Make sure that the area in which you are renovating has a large enough differential between the two- and three-bedroom properties and you have to pull off the renovation so that it looks like the extra room should be there. If you throw up a $5000 wall in the middle of a lounge room in a unit, don't expect your valuer to add $100 000 in value. However, it will improve the rental yield. You need to be clever. This strategy, combined with a rejuvenation, I believe will be the big winner for renovators, creating equity and a substantially higher rent.

$ *Revamp.* This strategy is really about looking at the properties you already hold in your portfolio. Maybe you have had them for a few years, you have had some growth, you have done a renovation and as they stand they are coasting along. You have the means and money to invest in another property but I encourage you to reassess your current portfolio as you may be leaving some money on the table. If you did all the research when you bought the property, then you know it is located where people want to live, you have had good growth and it has been a valuable addition to the portfolio. Now look at the comparison and advantages of using your equity growth for buying another property or refashioning the one you already have. You'll make a saving on stamp duty and purchase costs, which could take your current property to the next level.

For example, in one of my properties I could create a new bedroom complete with stairs in the attic for $35 000. This would bump the value up by $100 000. Or I could spend the same amount of money to purchase a $250 000 property and be able to cover a 10 per cent deposit and stamp duty. Where would my $35 000 be better spent? So don't forget your current portfolio. This might even mean looking at your home as a potential investment property if you move elsewhere. Remember, if the fundamentals of your home-cum-investment property do not get you to your goals, it is just a convenient and easy investment that may not get you ahead financially. I have seen clever owners negotiate with the body corporate to buy their ceiling space or even gain sole access to the roof in apartment blocks. Don't limit your thinking.

$ *Detonate.* Okay, so this is not an R, but I was a mining engineer specialising in explosives for more than 15 years so I can't help myself. This is not so much a strategy as a complete 'wipe from the face of the earth' and rebuild type of renovation. This might sound drastic and in my opinion many a home renovation would be very well placed to have this strategy applied to it. Clients of my mortgage business time and time again spend more than $500000 refashioning their current home into a new home when a high-end, newly built home on the same block of land could cost less.

So, as an investor you may find a great location with a property that needs to be 'detonated'. Consider doing this and putting on a new project home, relocatable home or similar. Be aware, though, that if a lender takes security over an asset — that is, a property on land — to lend you money and then you bulldoze the house and leave just the land it leaves them exposed so they will want to know about it if they have lent you more than the value of the asset. This strategy is a bit drastic and will require lengthy council approvals and a high capital cost to build a new house, but there is opportunity — especially if you are buying the property at land value. And, of course, the rental yield and tax deductions will be higher on a new property.

These, essentially, are the renovation types you can employ. At a high level most renovators are split between cosmetic and structural renovation. This is usually a function of how much money they have available to contribute and how much risk they are willing to take on. In my experience the 'repair' strategy is where most property investors start as they build up their portfolio and once they have funds available to contribute they move to the 'rejuvenate' strategy.

Only a few people have stumbled upon the amazing opportunity of the 'restructure with a twist' strategy and very rarely does an experienced property investor consider the revamp — but they should, especially as they reach their borrowing limits.

It could be that the 'detonation' strategy is the only strategy you use when looking for properties at or below land value in good areas. It all comes down to what suits you and your budget, and what you want to achieve.

Renovating is going to cost you money and time so you need to know how to assess properties with your strategy, your budget and your outcome in mind. We are going to look at this in the next chapter.

CHAPTER 17

Costing your renovation

Costing the renovation and knowing what to spend is difficult as everyone has a slightly different strategy and end game. However, from teaching renovation as a path to prosperity for many years I have found that everyone always wants a rule of thumb. People have different ways of working out the rule of thumb as to how much they should spend on a renovation. They are all right. So for what it's worth, I am going to work through some general rules of thumb for your cosmetic renovation assuming that you will not be selling the property at the end. The reason I am going to go through the workings, and not just give you a hard and fast rule but show you the workings to apply, is so you can then change the figures to suit you.

First you need to work out what the purchase price should be so you know whether you should even consider purchasing the property. I have read a lot of books and been to many courses and I can tell you that the figures vary. With that in mind, let's work through how you need to work it out to come up with your own rule. It all starts and ends with the numbers.

$ Work out what the median price is in the area, visit the relevant properties and note the improvements.

$ Calculate the cost of the improvements on the property you have selected.

$ Calculate the buying and holding costs to cover the period while you're renovating.

Then, based on the asking price, you can work out the profit. You get to set the profit that suits your needs so that you can reach your goals in the time frame you have predetermined. You want, at the very least, to get every dollar you spent recouped. So if you spend $20 000, you want to add $20 000 in value. However, your goal is to make money, and that does not make you money. You need to create more value than what you spend. If you are merely restumping, reroofing and fixing cracks in the wall, I doubt you're going to get any of your money back. Your work will simply enable the property to remain standing.

Some people say you need to make $2 for every $1 you spend, others say $3. You just need to be realistic. Obviously, if you spend $20 000 and create a further $20 000 in value, the property will be worth $40 000 more than your purchase price; that is, you will have made $2 for every $1 you spent ($40 000 ÷ $20 000). This gives you an idea of a rule of thumb you might consider for the profit you want to generate.

Generally, the rule of thumb on how much you should spend on a renovation ranges from 8 to 10 per cent of the purchase price. Some renovators believe they can do a rejuvenation renovation — that is, a new kitchen and bathroom — for 8 per cent of the purchase price. Others allow this to creep a little higher. I would normally aim for the 10 per cent mark when doing big-picture guesstimates and if you are a first-time renovator I would suggest you aim for 15 per cent on the purchase price as a return; that is, $2.50 for every dollar you spend.

How can you do a big-picture calculation to work out whether there will be a profit? There are many methods: you can work your way up from the asking price or work your way down from the median as we did in the flipping strategy.

Involve the professionals

Some people, when planning a renovation, take an extra precautionary step. They contact a valuer to not only assess current market value but also to assess the potential market sale price *after* renovations.

For this, you would prepare a comprehensive list of the improvements you intend to carry out and request an estimate of the valuation once the work has been completed. This will not be a definite guarantee of valuation until the work is complete, but it gives you an appraisal.

In this way you know exactly how much the completed renovation would bring and from that you can determine how much you're prepared to pay for the property in order to receive a margin for profit. This highlights the need for finding sufficient differential between improved and unimproved properties in the target area. There is no point taking a project on if your improved value equals your costs.

So the support of professionals is important. Most people have trouble conceiving the finished product with makeovers. You need some skill here. Look for an interior designer who has experience with investor renovations. Experience counts a lot, as does getting the right people around you. You don't want to renovate too much or too little.

Renovate for profit

The final word on the concept of renovation for profit is the definition of profit. We have looked at the actual profit for a flip and we have discussed the return on a renovation: in the order of $2.50 to $3.00 for every dollar you spend.

Unlike for the flipping strategy the 'profit' of your renovation is not going to go directly into your bank account. You need to access this new value via a loan and more than likely you will be limited to 80 or 90 per cent of the value you have added. However, you will only be able to actually access this profit if you can afford to service all the debt. Lenders need to know you can afford to pay them back. For some people, serviceability will be the limiting factor so you can only have one property at a time and the flipping strategy may be your only alternative: one property at a time making some money to build your nest egg so you can get to the point where you can buy the property you want to hold for the long term — this may be your home or even your future home.

Work your numbers down

Let's examine the steps for working back from the median to develop a rule of thumb. This rule of thumb will enable you to quickly look at any property and calculate — based on your 10 per cent budget — the percentage profit and percentage costs of the purchase price, so that you can determine what the purchase price of your property should be.

Step 1

Determine what the median property looks like; that is, define what the median in the area physically looks like. Get on websites, key in the median price in your selected area and see what pops up. The median property may, for example, be a three-bedroom rendered house.

Step 2

Look at price points 20 to 30 per cent below that median price for that type of property. You may consider yourself a good negotiator, in which case you may look at properties 10 per cent or even 15 per cent below the median with the view of negotiating down further from the asking price. As you will see later, you will need the value of the property after renovation to be worth 35 per cent more than the purchase price.

Step 3

If you take the 20 to 30 per cent below median figure, pick a midpoint and apply the 10 per cent renovation costing rule.

Step 4

Consider acquisition (or buying) costs, stamp duty, transfer fees, mortgage registration, legal fees, disbursements and loan set-up costs including lender's mortgage insurance (if LMI is paid in cash, not from the loan or other borrowings). Stamp duty will vary from state to state.

Step 5

Add your finance costs. These are time-dependent so first you have to know what you plan to do with the property in terms of renovating and how long it will take. The finance costs are the payments you have to make for as long as the property is untenanted.

Step 6

You need to know how you're funding this purchase. If you're using a line of credit to contribute the deposit and the acquisition costs, you're essentially borrowing 100 per cent plus costs. As you will see in table 17.1 this means your loan is 106 per cent of the purchase price. If you're also using borrowed funds from a line of credit for the renovation, you need to include the interest cost on that as well, which means you're paying interest of 116 per cent.

This means that some of the funds will have to come from elsewhere — for example, your home or savings — and the majority of the funds will be borrowed against the property you're buying. That is, you may have 5 per cent,

10 per cent or 20 per cent coming from one property, and the balance of 95 per cent, 90 per cent or 80 per cent respectively secured against the new property. If you're borrowing the 6 per cent acquisition costs and 10 per cent renovation costs, these will come from the equity you have accessed from your home.

Let's work through an example to clarify this.

Example

Assume David was looking to buy in an area where the median price for the suburb is $550000. He starts looking at properties 20 to 30 per cent below the median with the plan of renovating to the standard of a median priced property. The properties are valued between $385000 and $440000 and he takes a midpoint of $410000. He plans on spending six months doing the renovation and he will spend 10 per cent of the purchase price, returning 15 per cent of the purchase price.

The finance costs are based on your specific circumstances. It's possible you may be borrowing up to the full 116 per cent.

To see how this affects the calculations and to download a spreadsheet, go to my website at <www.yourpropertysuccessnow.com.au/ypsbookbonus>.

Enter your own numbers so that you're not stuck with rigid formulae that someone else has given you.

This example is based on borrowing all the funds for the purchase — that is, you make no contribution from savings. Have a look at table 17.1.

Table 17.1: calculating the end value required

		As a percentage of the purchase price
Median	$550000	
Estimated purchase price	$410000	100.0
Renovation cost	**$41000**	**10.0**
Stamp duty, transfer and registration fees	$20905	
Legal fees	$1500	
Disbursements	$1000	
Finance fees	Nil	

(continued)

Table 17.1: calculating the end value required (*cont'd*)

		As a percentage of the purchase price
Total acquisition costs	$23 405	6.0
Finance cost and renovation taking 6 months ($2 965 × 6)	$17 790	4.3
Total costs	$82 195	20.3
Profit margin calculated as a percentage of purchase price	$61 500	15.0
Total costs plus profit margin		35.3

Note: Interest rate used is 7.5 per cent p.a.

Table 17.1 shows how you work out your costs as a percentage of the purchase price. If you were looking at a property on the market at $500 000 and you were using borrowed money to fund everything, then to make a 15 per cent profit margin the end value of the property would need to be 500 000 × 135.3 per cent; that is, $676 500.

You have created a rule of thumb specific to your requirements. If you contribute the deposit from savings and you're interested in a property priced at $250 000 you would need to have it valued at $336 000 (250 000 × 134.4) in order to make a 15 per cent profit. This figure of 134.4 per cent comes from the spreadsheet on the website.

There's not much difference in the cost as a percentage between the two scenarios. In fact, if you were to contribute the renovation costs, acquisition costs and a 20 per cent deposit from savings, the figure drops slightly to 34 per cent. So you can create your own rule of thumb. That way you can quickly look at a property and do the calculation. If the asking price is $250 000 and you renovate at a cost of 10 per cent of that price, you need to have an end value worth 135 per cent of that.

 Toolbox tip

You don't have to renovate straight away. You may decide to postpone renovations until you have the money and rent the property out.

Using table 17.1 you can work out your own figures so that you can allow extra time for planning and saving for the renovation and also work out how much you need to be setting aside each month from your pay to cover finance holding costs when you do renovate.

This gives you your own rule of thumb and, in effect, it works in two ways. You know that your costs will be 35 per cent above the purchase price or 135 per cent of the purchase price. However, you can also turn the equation on its head by looking at the medians in the area and working out what your target purchase price should be. For instance, if the median is $400 000: 400 000 ÷ 135 per cent is $296 000. You can work out very quickly how much you need to pay for a property to make the profit margin you want. Combine this with the budget of 10 per cent for the renovation — that is, $29 000 — and what the renovation requirements are and you can quickly work out whether there is a deal to be had. For instance, will the $29 000 allow you to complete all the works required to bring the property to the standard of a $400 000 property?

 Toolbox tip

You might accept a lower profit margin on a renovation. Some people do this by sacrificing profit for future growth. For instance, a new, anticipated infrastructure announcement will enable you to resell the property in two years at a great profit based on the expected capital growth. Remember, you would at the very least get a higher rent for your efforts. You therefore sacrifice immediate benefit, but the higher rent is helping your cash flow while you wait for that announcement. In this case you may try to minimise your renovation budget and concentrate on the properties that only need the 'repair' or 'refresh' strategy. Your budget would then be closer to 3 or 5 per cent of the purchase price. If you are planning a renovation at a cost of 10 per cent of the purchase price, and returning a profit of 15 per cent of the purchase price with acquisition and holding costs of 10 per cent, then the property you buy needs to go up in value 35 per cent more than you paid for it.

By adding this quick rule of thumb to your buying criteria checklist you can readily evaluate any property within minutes. Before you even start looking at a property physically you can work out whether you should waste time visiting it or not.

Visit <www.yourpropertysuccessnow.com.au/ypsbookbonus> and download a spreadsheet so you can work out your own numbers.

You now know how to work out whether there's money in the deal. In chapter 10 we discussed how to narrow the approximately 12 000 suburbs and towns throughout Australia down to three areas to search in. In chapter 13 we learned how to assess the actual properties for renovation when you do visit them.

Renovations are fraught with budget overruns and time-frame blowouts, and there are many opportunities to learn. I think they call these 'character building'. After many renovations I have found there are things that work and things that don't. Next I am going to share with you some of the things that I have learned along the way.

CHAPTER 18

My tips, mistakes and recommendations

I am going to share some of my renovation experiences and those of my students and mortgage broking clients. You don't often hear about the mistakes that people make, and in many cases a great new technique is invented from a mistake or 'learning opportunity'.

The information and photos of my own renovations in this chapter should serve as a resource for you. It includes not only individual rooms, but also some of the important areas in and around your property.

When I started writing the chapter, I intended to share a few tips, but as I got into, the list of tips grew and grew to the point where there were too many to include in a book. Rather than fill the book with dot points I chose a few tips for each section. I urge you to check out my website at <www.yourpropertysuccessnow.com.au/ypsbookbonus> for many more tips, mistakes and recommendations.

Finding a property and then assessing it for renovation potential is only half the battle. Once you've bought the property, you then need to act quickly to organise your renovation. Planning your renovation and then carrying out the renovation are the final keys to a renovation success plan.

Before you begin

Before you start renovating, get a quantity surveyor to do a scrapping schedule. This will enable you to get immediate tax deductions for the life of the products you are removing, which will help with the cash flow. Speak to your accountant as you may find that the property has to be rented first, before you can get the ATO to accept the scrapping schedule.

Always consider the risks: what you're going to do if things go wrong and how you're going to cover yourself. Have plan B ready to go. This includes anything from having income protection insurance in case you're injured and can't work, to having a plan to rent a property that you considered flipping. Or even a strategy to sell quickly if you need to.

Write out your specifications on a per room, per trade basis. This means your quotes compare apples with apples and you can manage variations easily.

Where possible, get a fixed-price contract. In some instances this is not possible; for example, when your carpenter is replacing a few pieces of rotten floorboards.

Always include in your letter of offer that you want access prior to settlement so you can get quotes organised and finalised. That way you'll be ready to go as soon as you get the keys.

Bang for your buck

Whether you're reselling your property, flipping or accessing equity to purchase again, you need to know where the bang for your buck is. It's important to prioritise where the greatest added value can come from.

First impressions

First impressions are so important. Think about how you want to feel when you see and walk into a house you may be living in soon for the first time.

The outdoor area is the first impression for tenants and—most importantly—for the valuer, so clean up, paint the exterior and mow the lawn. Attach or paint on the street number, replace the mail box if necessary and make sure the front door is attractive.

You may pay $500 for a garden clean-up and some new plants, but it will make a huge difference in terms of first impressions. If you want to go all out, you'll pay between $5000 and $15 000 for new fencing and landscaping.

The entry is the first impression of the inside of the house—make it uncluttered and welcoming. As you can see in figure 18.1, renovating an entry can be a very worthwhile makeover.

Use colour creatively. If the entry is dark, consider an optical illusion and use half-strength paint colour in this area to give the appearance of it being lighter.

Figure 18.1: entry area before (left) and after (right)

Floor plans

Your floor plan is the key to what you can do cosmetically, so manipulate and maximise this to add value. Look at adding or converting under-utilised space into a bedroom or removing walls between the kitchen, dining and even living areas—as long as they are not structural changes. Remember that structural = $$$.

Adding a hallway door will cost about $500, but it can save in heating costs. In the second photo in figure 18.1 you can see the 'finished' look a hallway door and some built-in bookcases can give.

Painting

Painting is probably going to give you the greatest bang for your buck. It will refresh the property immediately and give it a light, bright and clean feel. If you are delaying your renovation until you get funds, this is one thing you should consider doing during the first year or so. In figure 18.2 (overleaf) you can see what a difference a paint job has made to one of my own investment properties.

When getting painting quotes make sure they include preparation. I once thought I had received a bargain quote only to find out the hard way that it did not include preparation. They even painted over the top of spider webs! So you have to decide whether you want to do the preparation or you want to pay for it to be done. It will take a painter less time, but it does add to the quote, especially for an older property. Allow between $5000 and $10 000 for painting indoors and outside.

Figure 18.2: one of my investment properties before (top) and after (bottom)

Skylights

First and foremost use paint to create a light, bright, clean space. If that isn't enough, you can add immediate natural light with skylights. But ensure you comply with your council's regulations. For one of our renovations the council's regulations stated we could have three skylights, not visible from the street and less than one square metre in size each. Skylights cost between $800 and $3000 installed. Figure 18.3 shows one that I had installed in the kitchen of one of our investment properties.

Figure 18.3: a skylight brings extra light into an area

Bathrooms and kitchens

When renovating for profit, bathrooms and kitchens provide great value-added outcomes.

Bathrooms

The bathroom in one of my properties was quite small (1.36 metres wide) so I replaced the tiles with rectangular ones measuring 600 mm × 300 mm that run the length of the bathroom. Have a look at figure 18.4.

Figure 18.4: a 1.36-metre wide bathroom goes from cluttered (left) to spacious (right)

For a lower-end renovation a fresh, funky shower curtain is good value for about $25.

Remember to consider clever concealing ideas in a practical way before carrying them out. It may look fancy to hide the toilet cistern behind tiles, but when there's a leak you may have access problems due to the tiling.

For a bathroom renovation allow anywhere between $1000 (for a new vanity and fixtures) and $15 000 (for a whole new bathroom).

Kitchens

Most kitchen improvements usually offer high returns. The smaller your investment, the higher the potential for recovering costs. Avoid budget-breaking extras such as state-of-the-art cooktops, ovens or premium benchtops. However, I would include these if you are flipping as in that case your market is mainly owner-occupiers looking at better quality finishes.

Buyers will pay special attention to cleanliness, layout and storage capacity. A kitchen renovation can cost anywhere between $1000 and $20000, so consider your options carefully. You may find that paying $500 to replace the cupboard door handles and giving the kitchen a good clean does the job.

Consider using 100 mm × 100 mm glass tiles, compliant with the required safety specifications, behind the stove. Glass splash backs are great, but expensive. For the same cost I had glass tiles applied to an entire kitchen area. See figure 18.5.

Figure 18.5: glass tiles can be a great and cheap alternative to a glass splashback

Fittings and fixtures

Always replace light switches if old and mismatched and power points when painting. After a new paint job there's nothing worse than refitting old gear.

Depending on the type of property, new light and power switches throughout will cost approximately $750.

Don't use expensive fittings and fixtures. Tenants don't always treat your property well so look for durable brands and decent warranty periods. Do ensure that the renovation fits with the standard you are renovating to. This goes for lights, door handles and even the quality of doors.

Post-renovation

So now the renovating is over! But now comes the most important part of the renovation: finding out how much value it has added to your property.

Valuing the renovation

The valuer is the most important person in your renovation with regard to your releasing equity strategy. You need to finish your renovation and then concentrate on a plan regarding the valuer and valuation. This is the key to your success.

The day before the valuer comes, check the street. You may have to get out there to clean up litter and mow the nature strip. Then make sure the first impressions of the house, outside and inside, are ideal. In fact, we even mow the common areas outside our neighbours' house to show the best possible streetscape to the valuer.

Property managers and tenants

Make sure the property managers you choose are self-motivated and willing to put a bit of thought behind their management. I have had to pay for an electrician to fix a faulty oven just because the tenants couldn't find the main oven switch, which by law is on a separate power point located close by. This should be the first question the rental manager asks the tenant. Otherwise you might find that the $100 you negotiated off the oven price just got chewed up in an unnecessary call-out fee.

Then there was the agent who, each November, needed reminding that the tenants were overseas students who would leave for the best part of two months to go home. For four years she forgot to organise for them to pay their rent in advance to cover this period.

Or consider the agent who, after being told that I had—at great expense—installed smoke alarms with 10-year batteries (as I wanted to be sure that the tenants were always protected) authorised an electrician to change them three months later as part of their annual maintenance on smoke alarms. I suspect there's an electrician out there someone with my batteries in his house!

When you are leasing, ask to read a copy of the agent's rental advertisement before the tenant sees it. I often find mistakes and I usually rewrite it myself to emphasise the benefits of the location and the property, including that it is newly renovated.

'Wow' expenses

'Wow' expenses (my own term) come in various forms. They may:

$ be worth considering even though you may never have heard of them

$ be invisible and unprofitable

$ surprise you

$ be top value destroyers.

Worth considering

To make those people looking at renting or buying say 'wow', check out these bright ideas:

$ second showerheads — you'll pay an extra $200 for the extra point and nozzle

$ under-cupboard kitchen lights and lights behind frosted cupboards (allow $500)

$ wardrobes at $1500 each

$ extra cleverly concealed storage under stairs, under kickboards in kitchens, or in the roof via the ceiling through an attic ladder ($1500)

$ the little things that make life easier, such as automatic garage doors or a garbage bin built into a benchtop.

The list goes on and is limited only by your imagination (and pockets!).

Unseen and unprofitable

These are not-so-nice, potentially expensive wow costs because you often won't notice them (although a property inspector should) and when you get the bill to fix them you will say 'wow'. They include roofs with leaks and rotting areas, dangerous insulation, sloping walls and floors, old circuitry and copper pipes, leaking window frames, pest damage and anything structural.

Surprise costs

These costs will wow you when you get the bill if you're not aware of them in advance:

$ replacing doors

$ removal of rubbish

$ not factoring in your own time

$ holding costs

$ the cost of delays

$ the cost of getting council approvals

$ variation of works (you may not have been specific enough in the work that you required, or the scope of work may have changed)

$ plumbing and electrical costs.

Value destroyers

These value destroyers will make you go wow when you go back over your renovation in a few years' time:

$ over-capitalising; that is, creating the best house in the worst street, thus exceeding the median value for the area

$ decorating to your taste

$ poor workmanship

$ delays

$ getting emotional and renovating for your dream home, not the renovation specifications.

Visit <www.yourpropertysuccessnow.com.au/ypsbookbonus> to see all my other 'gems'. As you can imagine, I add to these all the time, so revisit the website regularly.

In summary, there are many mistakes you can make while looking for opportunities through renovating a property. However, there is much to be gained. Getting the appropriate type of renovation completed on time and on budget will make you money and assist you in growing your property portfolio.

Although these mistakes have been fun to review (well, maybe for you but they still make me cringe), there are some general renovating tips that will show you where you can make money and what to avoid. We will have a look at these now.

CHAPTER 19

Organising the renovation

You've completed your renovation research and you've decided you're interested in doing a quick cosmetic renovation on your property. You probably have about six weeks between the time your offer is accepted and the day of settlement so now is the time to start preparing for the renovation.

You are wearing an investor's hat so this is not a time to get emotional or fall in love with the property. Don't let your heart rule your head. This is purely business.

Indeed, some people include having access to the property before settlement for the purpose of getting quotes as a condition in their letter of offer (as we read earlier). Your letter of offer could also request access to actually do renovations. This is risky and may be a deal breaker for the vendor because if settlement does not go ahead they could end up with half a kitchen and you have wasted your money.

Getting started

There's plenty of number crunching and milestone planning involved in even the smallest renovating job. If you know exactly what you need to do and how you'll need to go about it, it will reduce your chances of the project going off the rails and taking longer and costing more than intended. Basically, you need to know how to organise a quick renovation.

Economise on materials

Shop around as you may be able to find discounts on some of the materials you need. Where possible, aim for materials that the supplier currently has in stock, preferably in surplus, as there is a far smaller chance of getting a discount when materials have to be ordered in. Only do this for tasks that you're confident you'll be able to do yourself, as some tradespeople won't use materials if they can't guarantee their quality. Carpet suppliers and Caesarstone providers often have leftovers from big jobs. Ask them what they have and what discount you can get. Consider looking in the local trading post or on eBay for bargains.

Go for quality where it shows

It's worth investing in decent quality finishing products such as paint and fittings, as these will be on display and take the brunt of the property's wear and tear. Save money in the long run by reducing the need for future touch-ups.

Get several quotes

When looking for professional trade help, get two or, better still, three quotes in order to give yourself a large enough sample to make an informed decision. Make sure one of them is a local.

Once you have three quotes it's time to get to work. Revisit your budget against the quotes and check that everything is still on track. If you realise your estimate for a particular job is way under the actual quote, decide whether that means you have to sacrifice something else. Once you are ready, check the tradespeople's references. You can even visit the site where they are currently working to check that they are qualified to do the work. For example, in some states plumbers must have specific licenses to do bathroom, laundry and kitchen renovations.

 Toolbox tip

List your renovation specifications and a complete scope of works by trade for each room. Assume nothing, specify everything. That way you have each trade quoting for the same thing and you'll be able to compare quotes easily. This also makes it easier for managing variations at the end.

Planning a renovation

Planning is vital not only for calculating budgets, costs, design elements and estimated finished values, but also because of the time factor. There are two things that bring a renovation plan unstuck:

$ getting emotional about the renovation and losing sight of the numbers

$ delays with tradespeople and materials.

It is one thing to calculate the cost of a renovation and what this will translate to in profit; it is another to actually do it. I am also guilty of getting bogged down and getting emotional — it happens.

You have looked at five tile shops you have quotes coming out of your ears. In addition all the colours seem to look the same. Then a clever salesperson shows you the ideal tiles in the perfect colour — but not at the perfect price. 'Surely an extra $5 per square metre is not such a big deal,' you say to yourself, and you buy them.

Decision made. Finally you are in a happy place. Mentally you have moved on to the carpet selection when the salesperson hands you your receipt and as you walk out the door you realise that the budget is blown. It happens: you could be tired, frustrated over it, or you may just have felt under pressure to make a decision.

There are no good excuses. Separate yourself emotionally from the renovation. And if you are tired, worn out or run down don't make the final decision — you may just need a walk around the block to regain perspective. Pull out the budget and make the decision: if you are overspending by $500 here, then where will you cut that from?

During our first renovation I fell for an amazing bath spout. This was pure indulgence with a $500 price tag. I had no more money. I could not cut anything from anywhere. I needed to find the extra money or I was not getting my spout. I convinced Todd to let me sell his old kitchen on eBay and keep the money. After all the builder was just going to pull it out and it would cost to cart it away in the skip. I got my spout. My plans to enjoy the extra-long bath were cut short with a move interstate and I can still remember my disappointment when I visited the property six months later to find the uni students were using the bath for storing their vacuum cleaner.

Even the simplest items can alter the cost-versus-value-added equation. When tiling the bathroom for example, you may 'love' the $124-per-square-metre imported Italian tiles, but the $15 tile will do the job just as effectively. You need to remember that it's an investment strategy and every cost needs to contribute to an overall return on investment.

You should be prudent about renovations. Although the colour of the bathroom in your investment unit may offend you, it only makes financial sense to change it if renovating the bathroom will stop the unit sitting vacant or lift the rent you can charge. Seek advice from your property manager and your tax accountant, and make a cost–benefit analysis of your proposed renovations. If the bathroom is going to cost $12 000 and you'll have to borrow the money and pay interest, but it will only add $5 a week to the rent, it's probably better left as is. You shouldn't over-capitalise by spending too much on renovations, or finishes and fittings. However, if it is going to add $40 000 in value and you can draw on that to contribute to your next property, it may be money well spent.

The second thing that can bring down any renovation is delays. This can come in many forms. Initially it can be that the tradespeople who said they would turn up to quote never did, or the carpenter had to pick the kids up from school as it was raining, or the electrician did not get his work finished so the kitchen can't go in and the kitchen installer's next available day is not until next week … and so it goes on.

According to HIA figures, the average completion time for a kitchen renovation has gone from 29 days in 2002 (September quarter) to 78 days in 2010. These increases present significant financial costs.

As the project manager of your renovation you simply have to deal with it. No matter how you plan your project — on paper, in Excel or in MS Project — you need to work in some contingencies. Yes, nearly everything that needs to be done is dependent on the thing before, so allow for a buffer of time in this instance when project planning.

When your builders tell you it will take five days, ask them if they are consecutive days. You may think that you will have the job done in five days — but they have other jobs and are planning on giving you a few days a week over the next fortnight.

Toolbox tip

As the project comes to a close you may find that your builder is on site less. He is probably doing quotes to line up his next job, which really should be done in his time (even if he is not on an hourly rate). If he is not on site, it can cause your time frame for completion to slip.

With building costs ever increasing and potential delays, you need to consider the effects of these on your renovation. During periods of slow capital growth, renovators will need to rely solely on improvements they've made to add value to their properties and not growth, if this is the case. Remember, even if one of the prongs of your Trident Strategy for low-risk property investing does not make you money, the other two will — just stick to the plan.

By the time you have the keys in your hand, you should have a completed renovation plan with estimated costs. You should then note down which tradespeople you need and plan who should do what. I then suggest you go through the property room by room and list down what each tradesperson will be doing. This then becomes the specifications that your tradespeople will quote to.

Each electrician is quoting on the same job. By all means ask them for suggestions. Remember these guys do this every day. If you have an image in mind, pull out a picture from a magazine to show them. Share the plan.

Once you have selected the tradespeople and confirmed their start dates you are ready to start sourcing and ordering the fixtures and fittings. Try not to have everything turn up at once. Have your deliveries arrive a few days before they are needed or people will be tripping over each other.

Toolbox tip

Check with the industry organisations in your state or territory for recommended contracts and requirements for warranty insurance.

You may decide that working and running a renovation site is too much for you. There are options: you could appoint the builder, for instance, as your project manager, but of course they will charge you a percentage for their work. Or you could appoint a project manager with their own team, but expect this to be 10 to 20 per cent of the building cost. An extra $5000 on a $50 000 renovation could be a good investment if it is saving you pain, stress and worry!

Only once you have your tradespeople ready and appointed and the fixtures and fittings ordered can you have a few days' rest before it all starts in earnest.

Toolbox tip

Think about this: anyone looking to rent usually needs to give two weeks' notice, so if my renovation is going to take 10 days (with a bit extra allowed for issues), then I want my tenant to move in two weeks after settlement, minimising foregone rent and maximising the period over which I can claim the interest against my tax. Therefore the work needs to be done pronto!

Scheduling

There are some handy tips you may want to take into consideration to make the renovation flow a bit more smoothly. Some may also assist you in ensuring a practical order of tasks. For example:

$ Leave replacing your carpets or floor coverings to last as these will get trashed with everyone walking through the property.

$ Paint from the top down.

$ Finishes such as splashbacks for stoves and frameless shower screens can only be measured and fitted after the tiling is done so allow enough time to complete those jobs.

$ Don't try to complete one room at a time. Have your tradespeople do everything they can across the entire property while they are on site. Sometimes when they go off to 'do a quick job' they can be gone for weeks. I'm not exaggerating!

$ If you are living in the renovation be aware that paint and even waterproofing can have deadly fumes so don't plan to sleep in the property immediately after application.

$ Leave the landscaping to the end as you may find that it gets trashed with all the tradespeople and equipment moving through it.

$ Start and end by being nice to your neighbours. Take them a case of beer or a cake and let them know when you are starting and when you plan to finish. They will have their lives turned upside down as well for a while, so be considerate.

Toolbox tip

Do not underestimate the power of morning tea. It may be that only I have noticed this, but over the past 10 years, tradies' tastes appear to have become more refined and healthier. Gone are the coke and pie lunches. They are usually popping out for a skinny latte. When you mention you are getting coffee, you will be taking orders like a Starbucks café. The message is this: reward your workers. Even put on a barbecue when it is all finished just to say thanks—after all, you want them for the next project.

Planning and executing your renovation project is the final part of the renovation story—nearly. Remember that you are doing this to make money and add value so the final step is to find out how much value you have added.

People looking for a property to rent generally inspect it for less than 10 minutes so they often can't remember whether there were one or two wardrobes, a dishwasher, and so on. It is amazing how frequently—especially in a market where there is a shortage of rental properties—a renter signs a lease and moves in to find the doesn't have an item or a feature that's on their list of requirements. (Obviously, when there is an oversupply of rental properties these items become more important.) So don't stress if you can't afford all the little 'nice to haves' that you think renters want as they may not even notice them. As discussed, you are often renovating just for the valuation. The most important thing is that the valuer knows what to look for and will record it.

Summary

The potential summary list for this chapter is too long to contemplate, but let's get some pointers on the page.

$ Ensure your property is structurally sound before you start. Have it independently inspected because termites, rot, old wiring and old plumbing could easily add $25 000 in unforeseen extras.

$ Make sure that your design concept is top-notch — do not compromise on this. Check out trends in magazines and inspect properties in the price bracket or above that you are renovating to.

$ Make sure the working drawings and specifications are detailed and accurate. This will minimise costly variations.

$ Do not over-capitalise in middle markets as this can be an issue. There's no norm to this, but the usual caveats apply: work within a budget and keep an eye on resale prices in your immediate vicinity.

$ Remember that the kitchen and bathrooms are probably the most important areas of the house — at least for the renovating-for-profit strategy. When the market is performing well, costs can be recouped quickly. When the market is flat and there is renovation activity, buyers become more discerning so improvements can add value and act towards distinguishing a property from the rest. But you also can over-capitalise.

$ Remember that a cosmetic renovation strategy is not a full-blown structural renovation. It is mainly about a perceived value (not an actual value). Ensure that everything you do is a benefit that will derive a higher rental price or improved value. Fixing the old roof, replacing wiring, re-stumping and fixing white ant damage will arguably improve the value of a property but they are dollars spent without a direct reward or 'wow' factor. Would you rather spend $10 000 on a fancy new kitchen or on fixing the roof?

The renovation safety net

If you have followed the Trident Strategy for low-risk property investing, you have created for yourself a renovation safety net. Imagine this is your first property and you did not get a great discount and your renovation has a bit of a blowout and it all seems like you just missed out on making a profit. Take a deep breath. You've done well. You've started: you've done the work needed to find a property and you've worked through the renovation with your sanity intact. All these things are a great achievement. And if you have followed the process and you did the research and you identified an area of growth, then the safety net has worked as one prong of your strategy is still working for you in creating equity. Don't be too hard on yourself as most people who buy investment properties only start with one strategy to make money and when that fails they have no plan B.

Remember that it all started with developing your buying criteria. One of these was capital growth. For instance, you may be targeting areas with predicted capital growth expectations above 8 per cent per annum. Now, six months down the track, you have had your head buried in your renovation with only a cursory look at the market. Take a closer look. Expected growth has exceeded your calculations and that of the experts and you are closer to 10 per cent per annum growth so in that six months your property has gone up in value by 5 per cent. For a $400 000 property, that's $20 000!

It's the Trident Strategy for low-risk property investing in action. Even if you mess up, the safety net is there to save you. Thus, if you play it right not only do you have the opportunity to make money through the renovation and when you buy, but then capital growth although kicks in: k-ching, k-ching!

CHAPTER 20

Review, repair, repent and replicate

For years I taught using the cookie-cutter approach, which went something like this: the final step involves finishing up the renovation with the valuation, accessing the equity from your property and — well — moving on to the next property and building your portfolio. Then once you have your renovation strategy tested, move on and do it again.

However, after years of perfecting this, I realised there is another step.

The final step

That final step is essentially about getting over the renovation, learning from it, refining your techniques and taking time to do a review. As such, once you have completed your renovation it is time to step back and consider a few things.

Review the renovation

How did it go? Were you on time? Did you meet the budget or was there a blowout? Pull out your planned budget and your actual costs. What was the issue? How did you go in appointing the tradespeople? Would you change any of them if you had to? What did you learn about dealing with tradespeople and even through the quoting period? This is where you look at issues and things you've learned and you note them down for next time.

I think renovations might be a lot like pain. Apparently, pain is the only emotion you cannot physically relive. That is probably why women don't stop at one child, even after a difficult labour. With time, the memory of the renovation dims, so while it is fresh write it down.

Repair

This is all about recognising what you have learned from the review you have just done. Could the issues have been anticipated? How could you avoid this next time? Was there something at the beginning you left off your buying criteria checklist when you were looking for a property?

After my first renovation, I noted down that I would never buy in an area again that had a heritage overlay. The small, 10 cm × 20 cm exhaust flap for the rangehood took three months to be approved by council.

How well did you coordinate the trades? the schedule? what you bought? What would you change? I had one student who was well down the path of his renovation success journey doing a significant structural renovation for a quick flip. When he went back and revisited his renovation budget he found that he could have increased his profit by $30 000 with better planning. (Actually, he taught me about structural renovations so I am not sure whether he was the student or I was.)

Repent

You need to get over the mistakes — and quickly. Everyone makes them. Just learn from them. I had a purple feature wall in my first renovation. In my case I learned to keep colour schemes neutral, simple and the same for every property. So have a laugh about it and move on.

When looking at your investment property, look at where you wasted time and money. Look too at where your efforts paid off — perhaps by dramatically improving the rental yield or the assessed value.

There are always things to learn from each and every property renovation experience. But it is important to have your fundamentals in place and not to deviate towards the newest fad (such as mining town accommodation, or 'high yield' regional towns, unless that is your strategy).

Remember, it is important to buy, own and add value to the type of property that will be in continuous strong demand into the future: a good investment property is one that will always be in strong demand. Remember that home buyers purchase about 65 per cent of all properties on the market and they're the ones that push up property values. So having a property that would suit an owner-occupier but where a renter could live adds to your low-risk investing strategy.

Replicate

Okay. So the property is renovated; you have learned from your mistakes and now you're ready to move on. Oh, but you can't move on without money, so it is time to have the property appraised so you can access some cash.

It's all about the valuer

This may stretch your thinking: we are going to wrap up this whole renovation section to understand how you actually get recognition for the value you have added.

Who do you think I keep front and centre of my mind when I am renovating? Over the past eight years I have asked more than one thousand people who have attended my seminars this question and only a handful of people have answered correctly. (Hint: the title of this section gives this away.) Some say that you should renovate for:

$ yourself

$ the renter

$ the real estate agent.

In fact, the first person I think of is the valuer. The valuer is the person with the power to declare the value of the property and hence how much profit can be made and how much money is available to pull out.

When I am comparing the $25-per-square-metre tiles and the $75-per-square-metre tiles, I ask myself, 'Is this going to make a difference?' When I am looking at benchtops I ask myself, 'Will the valuer recognise the value?' Every decision comes down to what the valuer will see. They won't see exependiture associated with termite damage, new sewerage or new guttering. They just assume that the property is structurally sound.

Only after I have assessed every renovation decision through the valuer's eyes do I consider the next person I renovate for: the tenant. Will wardrobes make this easier to rent? What about security bars, Foxtel, furnishings? And so on…

Knowing how you access the equity so you can do it all again is one of the fundamental cornerstones of growing your property portfolio. We will look at this in the next chapter.

Getting value where it's due

There are many things you need to know about organising your valuation and the process involved. More often than not the valuer is going to be appointed to evaluate the value of your property by the lender. So they are in control. You need to gain control. First, make sure you are the contact person for the valuer. Not your agent or the tenant—just you. Even if you are interstate and can't make the valuation you need to tell them what you have done and offer to send some information to make their job easier.

Then you have to revisit the property, strip away all association with the property and view it as if you are at an inspection to look at the property for the first time.

First impressions count

You need to be making an impact straight away. Look at the property from the outside. Does everything look in order, clean, tidy and consistent with the rest of the street? Is there anything that looks a bit funny, strange, out of place—something that if you were inspecting the property you would think, 'Hmm, I should check that out'? Because if you are asking questions about the property, so will the valuer. Remember that you inspected more than 100 properties before buying the property you're renovating now. You know what to look for. The valuer has seen thousands so they really know what to look for. If you create any doubt or preconception in their mind, they will be in that mind space when they inspect the property.

For instance, if I notice that the garden is overgrown, the lawn is not cut and the front door is old and daggy I won't expect much when I walk in. So I will automatically go in looking for faults: messy painting, do-it-yourself tiling…you know what I mean. If everything looks right, then the valuer will think, 'I am in and out of here. I have a list of renovations that have been done. I just need to verify that back in the office where I can check comparable sales'.

You want the first impression to be consistent with the property standard and then you want to create the scene for the valuer. This means styling the property. Either bring in your own furniture or get a stylist to do it for you.

Make it look lived in. Make the valuer want to live there. They will tell you until they are black and blue that furniture will not influence the valuation. But imagine showing them an empty property and then showing them the same property furnished and decorated so that they can imagine themselves pulling off their shoes and enjoying a drink there at the end of the day. It is all in the mind and it should not influence the valuation, but you should be willing to try everything to gently encourage the valuer to value the property in your favour.

That's why I spend my money on the bang. I don't spend my money on wiring and plumbing because the valuer doesn't care about that.

The valuer's role

If you pay a valuer to come in (as opposed to getting a bank valuation), you will probably get 10 minutes of their time. They are just validating the fact that the place is as they assume it should be. If you have done a renovation, you need to point out the differences between the most recent sale price for the property and what you believe your property is worth. They need to understand why it is worth more. Then they go back to their office and do all the comparable sales based on the number of bedrooms, the size of the block and the standard of the finish. Their report actually ranks your property against other recent sales, stipulating whether it is superior or inferior with respect to a variety of categories. Be warned though if the valuer is appointed by the bank as part of your refinance then they are in there for no more than about seven minutes — tops. So make your time count. And also be aware that if they can't find three comparable sales, the lender will rarely lend you money. So, creating seven-bedroom university accommodation may not be in your best interest. In addition, when you come to sell your buyers will have trouble getting finance. Remember to have an emergency exit plan, which means owning a property that others find easy to purchase.

Controlling the valuation

Let's assume you purchased a property with a 20 per cent deposit and you paid $500 000 for it. You completed a renovation on the property and you want to move on to the next property. You bought well, given that you purchased in a suburb that has been going through some 'gentrification' — and continues to do so. Rental demand is high and auction clearance rates in the suburb are higher than average. You ask your local agent to assess the value of the property with a view for 'potential' sale. Their 'opinion' is that it is worth $705 000. They are sales people and this is not usually a true reflection of the market so you need to start your research and find out what you think the comparables are.

Based on our handy formula we know that if you spent 10 per cent of the purchase price you need to revalue at \$675 000 to generate a 15 per cent profit (\$500 000 × 1.35). That was the basis of your initial figures and you believe that is the fair value. Does this all translate to equity? Yes. But can you use this equity? It all depends.

It depends on how effectively you work with the valuer.

In most cases when it comes to accessing equity your lender will use an independent value or do a 'drive-by' valuation. Your job (so to speak) is to convince a valuer to provide you with a valuation that secures equity from the increased value of your property. So a drive by is not going to work for you. They need to see the renovation. Remember, if the bank orders the valuation they usually accept valuations up to six months old, therefore if you bought four months ago your lender may not consider another valuation necessary. You or your mortgage broker need to convince them that there is a need for it. That's how you get a new valuation within six months of buying the property.

You need to take a business-like approach to securing a valuation: a property that looks like a home that anyone would be happy to live in is generally going to attract a higher valuation than one that is in disrepair or untidy — or simply yuk!

A successful strategy should deliver you your expected value. The equity you created is \$175 000 which, at an LVR of 80 per cent, provides an accessible equity of \$140 000; that is, 80 per cent of \$675 000 (as we are maintaining an 80 per cent LVR) minus the original loan amount. This represents quite a healthy potential contribution to your next property.

Getting the valuation you want

Assuming the property is ready and you have organised the valuer, you now need to get your evidence and documentation together. If you can find a copy of a valuation, you will see what the valuer is looking for and essentially the template that they use. There is basic information on the property, size, title information, past sales data and more. You will also find physical attributes of the property, the number of bedrooms, the appearance and anything unusual and different from when it last sold. This is where you add the renovation works done so that there is comparison data.

This is also where you do the research on recent sales. The valuer may only have access to sales older than three months. If your area has been experiencing good growth, then you want newer sales to be on that list so you need to keep your eye on the market and record these sales as well. In your document you need a photo, the block dimensions and the property details; that is, the number of bedrooms, the quality of finish and the recent sale price. Then you need to rank your property against this as inferior or superior. Basically, you are writing your own valuation for the valuer. They will come up with their own conclusion, but you're having a major input in the process.

Toolbox tip

Be strategic about the properties you use to compare yours with. Obvious distressed sales are not going to do you any favours.

Visit <www.yourpropertysuccessnow.com.au/ypsbookbonus> to get a bonus copy of a sample template.

The valuer may ask you how much you spent and how much you think the property is worth. Through all your research and work, you have been able to deliver a superior result for less than what it should have cost. The valuer does not need to know you picked up the $125-per-square-metre mosaic Italian tiles for $17-per-square-metre from Grays online auctions.

You should hand the valuer the document you prepared, point out the major features and be elusive about the cost. Say that you are 'finalising figures' and 'still getting invoices in'. You suggest that the quotes you had ranged from $65 000 to $75 000 with builders but you project-managed the renovation yourself and could only really go on those estimates. Come up with ideas on how to deal with the question of how much the renovation actually cost, but don't give a figure. Also, you might point out that you were able to secure the property for $25 000 under market value based on the owners needing to sell, and the terrible state of the bathroom, roof, and so on.

When helping my sister get her property re-valued, we told the valuer there was terrible water damp (which was true) in the bedrooms and mould on the carpet, which scared most people away and that we believed that's why she was able to buy the property for $15 000 under market value, as could be seen clearly by what the median was and what she bought it for. In her case she was clever and, pre-auction, had her builder look at the property. He found that the guttering was leaking and that a fix would stop the water. With a good clean and time to dry out, the issue would be behind her. In fact she even met with one of the other owners in the block of apartments and along with her strata search she found that the body corporate had adequate funds in their sinking fund and no allocation for using them. Prior to purchasing the property she had the body corporate agree to fix the guttering. That was smart.

It's all about the perceived value, not the actual cost.

The valuer will start adding up the renovation value, the purchase price, even the discount value that you bought for under market value. They will not necessarily add on your 25 per cent increased value (that is, 10 per cent renovation cost and 15 per cent profit): you need to justify that. So point out the features, give them your document and when they ask you how much the property is worth tell them, 'about $685 000'. I usually also use rental appraisals and published rental returns for an area so that I can substantiate the value of the property.

Use rental returns to substantiate value. For instance, if a rental manager writes a letter saying that they could get $590 to $615 per week for the property, then take the $590 per week figure and check out the rental return for the area in the back of a property investing magazine. Assuming that the return is 4.5 per cent, then $590 × 52 gives a total rent of $30 680 per annum. As a 4.5 per cent return this makes the property worth $30 680 ÷ 0.045 = $682 000. Add this to your document along with the rental letter. If you use the higher rental figure the property is worth $710 000 so in your valuation document you could say that your expected valuation result is between $682 000 and $710 000. You could also work this out at 4 per cent per annum yield and 5 per cent per annum yield, showing various values.

By being conservative and having a lower yield, you will get an even higher value! So, as you were going to make a 15 per cent profit if the property valued at $675 000, anything more is just jam!

Toolbox tip

Add a little bit extra on top of your goal value as the valuer is a professional and they are not going to take your word for it. Indeed, in my experience, they reduce whatever you say the property is worth.

There you have it: a basic strategy that will get you to the price your property valued at, or even higher than what you started out with.

Toolbox tip

Let's say that the budget runs over and you need to be doing a lot to make up your profit. (And don't forget your capital growth safety net.) Check out what the growth rate has been in the past six months and apply that to your valuation template along with your evidence.

Once the valuer submits their report to the lender, the process of gaining access to the funds begins. We have covered this a few times in the book so glance back again on how this is done. Essentially, however, you will tap into your new equity so you can do it again — and again and again — or as long as you can afford to.

The renovation strategy and adding equity to your property is a quick way to propel you towards your goals. Combined with creating equity when you buy below the market and equity from capital growth, you have three sources of equity that your property can ride on and from where you can continue to build your portfolio. This is the Trident Strategy in action.

CHAPTER 21
My renovation examples

We have been renovating for more than 10 years and in some cases we have renovated the same property twice. As you can imagine, we have learned a lot and we've had plenty of opportunity to make money through renovation. I want to share with you a few of these renovations with different budgets and time frames so you can see what is possible.

First, I am going to share some that got away — luckily. I think Garth Brooks nailed it with his song title, 'Thank God for unanswered prayers'. Sometimes you just get too close and you miss the obvious. I know if we had not been so insistent on our research we would be in a whole different place today.

In 2002, when we first moved back to Sydney, my husband Todd and I were relentless in our pursuit of more properties. We were each searching for our next purchase and we had different budgets and buying criteria. As a result, every Saturday we had not four but six suburbs to cover — Maroubra, Manly, Mosman, Bondi Beach, Newtown and Balmain. For anyone who knows Sydney you can imagine the endless crises crossing the Sydney Harbour Bridge, and the timing issues. Regardless, we always managed to see 10 properties every Saturday and within three months we saw more than 170.

Saved by the building inspection

One property we were really interested in involved a restructure twist: turning four units — two downstairs and two upstairs — back into the original side-by-side terraces. In the lower north shore there was a real demand for these types of homes. All was on track until the building inspection.

We did a building inspection and found that the property required a minimum of a $100 000 in costs just to fix the concrete cancer and repair the walls that were slowly falling apart. We still turned up at auction. However, we worked this into our price. This was just after the first *The Block* television show and there was a group of young couples at the auction obviously keen to create a similar experience with their mates. The auction got to our limit and we stopped bidding. When they kept bidding it became obvious that they had not found the problems that our building inspector had. I imagine that was another renovation that ended in tears and maybe even a parting of friends.

It is one thing to share a bottle of wine with your friends and plan your joint multimillion-dollar property portfolio, but leave the dreams at the dinner party. I have seen many friends have fallouts over joint property purchases. Go in with your eyes wide open.

So you can see how important building inspections are.

Saved by the neighbours

We researched another property up for auction. Before we even got to look at the body corporate files a neighbour alerted us to the fact that the lift in the wonderful unit complex on Manly Beach needed rebuilding. The cost for each unit owner was going to be $20 000 and was required as a special levy within the next two months. So once again we worked that into our price. It became obvious that the young couple with a baby really wanted the property and as the bids slowed it became even more obvious that they were going to pull funds from credit cards to make the purchase. They were successful but I doubt they were aware that two months after settlement they were up for more money.

Saved by the strata inspection

On one occasion we found a great unit with amazing views. Through research we found that it was on the market for $550 000 and the owner had bought it for $600 000 only a year earlier. The market had not dropped so it seemed unusual. Whenever we asked the agent what the issue was he just replied, 'You have to make your own enquiries. Do your research.' So we offered $495 000 subject to finance, a pest and building inspection and all being in order after our enquiries and investigations. To our surprise, the offer was accepted. The expiration of our offer at 5 pm came and went and the agent wanted us to sign but the report on the body corporate was not in so we allowed our offer to expire.

Now, for someone to take a $100000 hit on their purchase within 12 months there had to be something to be worried about. Sure enough, at 8 pm the strata inspection report arrived. Although the building inspector had not found anything wrong with the apartment the report told the story of a building in trouble. Due to significant concrete cancer issues the property needed $2.1 million dollars spent on it to reroof and refix the property — yes, a lot of money.

This expense was to be spread across the 21 units in the block based on size, which would have meant a cost of $100000 for the owner of the unit we were looking at. These funds were going to be raised as a special levy within the next year. Phew! Tragedy averted. However, look at the twist: there were potentially going to be a lot of people selling their properties as they could not raise the funds. In fact, this could have been an amazing opportunity if you were willing to take on the risk. Moreover, the agent was not surprised when we pulled out. He didn't even ask why. Do you think he knew?

Toolbox tip

If you are buying a property within a body corporate get a professional to do a review of the files for you and give you a report. No questions — just do this. Once you have a report to use as a template, you can see what they highlight and the headings they use. Then you can attempt to do this review yourself. That is, make an appointment with the strata manager's office and review the files. I err on the side of caution and review at least five years' worth. If you cannot go to the strata manager's office to do the inspection, often your solicitor can organise this to be done for you. Just make sure you get it done.

The following are actual renovations we have completed. Visit my website <www.yourpropertysuccessnow.com.au/ypsbookbonus> for a full breakdown of works and costs.

First purchase, first success

Our property journey started in 2000. After a year of reading books and going to seminars Todd and I applied all the research on locating properties we had learned and combined it with our low-risk investing strategies. We bought our first properties in Melbourne on St Patrick's Day 2001.

After months of getting to know our selected suburbs we found what we thought was a great opportunity. There were a few twists involved. We found two properties on separate titles being sold side by side at the one auction. That is, instead of saying, 'Going once, twice, sold for $400 000' the price was $900 000. Hence we could each buy one in our own name. Figure 21.1 shows what they looked like.

Figure 21.1: our first purchase in Melbourne

Yes, they were two of those beautifully built, 1860 period properties, and they were pink. What's more, due to the heritage overlay, it took six months for the council to approve the colours we requested.

Finally, a colour scheme. You would have thought they may have accepted the four National Trust colour schemes we submitted — that would have made sense — but they did not.

My first property was purchased for $425 000 and gobbled up my entire savings of $45 000. Straightaway I had to hand over $25 000 from my $45 000 for stamp duty and I was left with a 5 per cent deposit. So the first property was bought with a 95 per cent loan.

I funded the renovation with a $50000 personal loan. I knew exactly how long it would take, how much it would cost and what the property would be worth at the end. Nine months later it was valued at $700 000. So I had increased the value of the property by $275 000 in nine months with a $50 000 renovation. This meant I had returned $5.50 for every dollar I spent on the renovation!

By now you would know that was not all due to renovation; it was a combination of buying below the market — that is, we bought two properties at once at a discount — and there was capital growth. The renovation itself only took six months. It took a bit longer to organise the valuation.

I had to make a significant amount of money and that was about getting it right the first time. It was not about being lucky or buying at the right time; it was about all the hard work and a year of planning in finding the property and renovating it to the right standard, on budget and on time. From there I developed my Trident Strategy for low-risk property investing.

The best thing about that purchase was that we bought with a twist in mind. We bought two at once — converting one from commercial premises — we renovated to a high standard and we added value through renovation. Although we bought two properties, we did not just increase the property value by $275 000. Todd completed the renovation on his property as well, increasing the value even more on his property. Fast forward to 2012 and the properties are worth $2.5 million combined.

 Toolbox tip

Renovation is a tool you can use to create equity and increase rental yield. The smaller the cost between your costs to hold a property and the income you earn on it, the more properties you can acquire. It is a way you can create a balance in your portfolio.

Not only did we increase the value of the properties, and put ourselves in a position to release equity, but we also significantly increased the rent.

In summary

The renovation was a great success. It enabled me to refinance to an 80 per cent LVR straightaway and pull out equity to buy again. In hindsight if I had received better advice I would have kept the LVR higher at 90 per cent and had more funds to buy a third property sooner.

Toolbox tip

Couples should buy in individual names first before buying together. It may increase your buying power and have tax benefits, specifically land tax.

The bathroom in figure 21.2 used to be a bedroom.

Figure 21.2: the renovated bathroom and 'that' $500 spout

Notice the two shower heads in figure 21.3!

Figure 21.3: notice the double shower

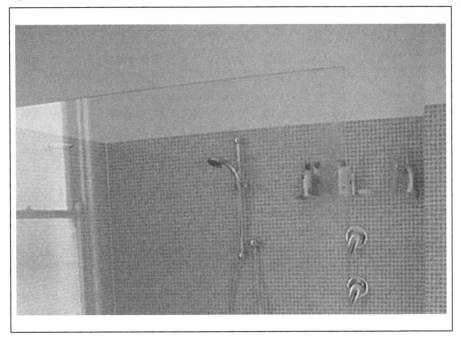

Visit my website at <www.yourpropertysuccessnow.com.au/ypsbookbonus> to see more of the renovation photos and a breakdown of the costs.

The $14 000, 10-day renovation

This sounds tight, you say. How can you organise a renovation in 10 days? You now know the answer: the renovation was organised in the six weeks between contract and settlement. It was only executed in 10 days.

You may also be wondering, how can you make so much? Well, as you now know, value is not just delivered via the renovation and the timing. And it is not capital growth alone. We also added equity by buying well below the market value. Sounds like the Trident Strategy in action, doesn't it?

It was a really quick little renovation. It was a unit that we bought in Kingsford in Sydney.

When you find yourself as a property investor, you've gone through the process of doing all this research, and you've then completed a renovation, you look back on the past six months of your life and think, 'Do I have friends?' You haven't spoken to anyone in six months. You ask, 'What am I going to do with my weekends now?' You pick up the paper and say, 'Oh, why don't I go and have a look at a few properties?' That's what happened to us. And so, one Saturday in 2004 Todd was looking at properties in the paper.

We weren't looking at buying a property. We just had nothing to do that day, so we wandered down to Kingsford, thinking that it was a good opportunity to look around. Todd had been watching the suburb of Kingsford on and off. It is nestled between Coogee, Randwick and Kensington. The median values of all of those surrounding suburbs was at least $300 000 more than Kingsford so he predicted the trickle effect: property values would go up due to demand from purchasers no longer able to rent or buy in the neighbouring suburbs.

Anyway, we wandered down and had a look at four units. Remember that we were used to looking at 10 properties in one day and rushing around, so this really was a relaxing morning. They were all on the market for approximately $420 000 but we saw one in particular that we liked the best. We thought, 'This is the nicest. It's cluttered, but it's got a nice outlook'. And we walked away.

Three weeks later, Todd said, 'You know that unit for $420 000? All the others have come down to about $410 000. This unit's come down to $360 000.' We went back to have a look, couldn't find anything wrong with it, did the checks and research, found out what the person had bought it for (which was a lot less than the current price tag) and faxed over our offer. The agent told me I was rude and my offer was obscene. It was for $310 000.

I said, give the offer to the owner and see what they think. We weren't prepared to offer any more. The owner came back and said, 'Sure. I bought it for $200 000 for my kids when they were at university. I live overseas. Interest rates are going up. They've finished university now. Agent Rick thinks it is worth $400 000. I bought it for only $200 000. I'm going to make $110 000. I've made heaps of money. That's fine. I accept the offer.'

The property had comparable units selling for $410 000 and we bought for $310 000. We spent 10 days on the renovation. It only needed to be refreshed with a new kitchen and painting so we spent less than 5 per cent on renovations. We had early access to get quotes and show the property and had it rented before we even settled. The agent informed the renters of the renovations that we were planning to do. Figure 21.4 shows before and after photos of the kitchen.

Figure 21.4: the kitchen, before (top) and after (bottom)

In summary

The property was bought for $310 000 with an 80 per cent loan against it and all the remaining funds required were taken from a line of credit secured against another property, so we got a 110 per cent loan all up. We had the selling agent give us a realistic valuation straightaway (he knew we were not going to sell). So it was valued 10 days after purchase at $450 000. Based on the figures it continues to go up in value, it is always tenanted and it costs us nothing because it is positively geared. Even if you estimate that the true value was comparable at $410 000, our renovation of $14 000 got the property to a $450 000 valuation — even that is a good 10 days' work.

Beachside pad tidy-up

This one was a pleasure. It was renovated so that we could increase the rent. As with most of our renovations, to save money we lived in the renovation while we completed it. Living on a beach-facing unit on Bondi Beach was no hardship over winter. In fact we realised that we could take our time over this renovation when the tenants gave notice as we knew that the key time to rent a beachside property was not during the winter months. We had six months to complete what could have been a much shorter renovation.

In this three-storey block of 12 units, six of the units actually faced the ocean. The way they had been designed was that the main bedroom was the one room with a view. An architect had owned the property before us and had done some structural changes, including moving the kitchen to the back of the unit so that the kitchen and living areas benefited from the view and position. However, for some reason no-one seemed to know that our unit was different from the others. As we had been looking in the area for three months we had seen another unit in the block and that's how we knew.

Thus, when everyone else was using the last sale in the block as a comparable price we knew this unit was worth a lot more due to the $50 000-plus that had been spent on its reconfiguration — moving the bathroom to the back and the living zone to the front. Yet it was selling at the same price as the others, which didn't have those structural changes. You can see the kitchen and lounge in figure 21.5.

Figure 21.5: beachfront living on Bondi—our retirement home

In summary

We increased the rent by 24 per cent and the unit has never been vacant. We recognised that it had already had a major part of the renovation done, and that this had not been factored into the purchase price. In fact, people with renovation strategies often pass up opportunities because they don't know how to renovate a property, when they could be using their renovation knowledge to recognise a property that has been renovated but where the value has not been reflected in the price. The goal was to improve the rental yield with a few minor changes including replacing a Japanese-style sliding door with a wall to make a second bedroom and installing an internal laundry.

Renovating with a structural twist

I confess I am borrowing this renovation story from my sister Peta. However, I am telling you about it so you can see the benefit of adding bedrooms to a property. After months of research, this unit appeared advertised as an 80-square-metre, two-bedroom unit, which seemed really big. When we started playing with the floor plan it became obvious that a third bedroom could be added. Renovated three-bedroom units in the suburb were selling for $80 000 to $100 000 more than two-bedroom units. So there was opportunity.

She purchased the property with a 95 per cent loan and with the value that was created by buying below market value. (You will remember I mentioned earlier that this was due to the rising damp.) She waited while the capital growth of the area continued and more value was added. Then she started to get quotes for the work to be done. She went to the bank with the fixed price contract of $35 000 and asked for the funds. The property was remortgaged to a 90 per cent LVR and she used the borrowed funds to renovate. See the floor plan in figure 21.6. The kitchen was moved into the living area and it became the third bedroom. The valuer said that if she had only added a wall at the far end of the living area then it would not have justified the price increase of $100 000. As the new bedroom was actually an established brick-build room, he believed that future valuers would not realise that it was previously a two-bedroom unit.

In summary

The property was purchased for $456 000. Six months later it was valued at $525 000. After the $35 000, six-week renovation it was valued at $615 000. This property can now be rented for $200 per week more than it could prior to the $35 000 renovation. It had a great floor plan, making it possible to add a bedroom.

Figure 21.6: the floor plan pre-renovation

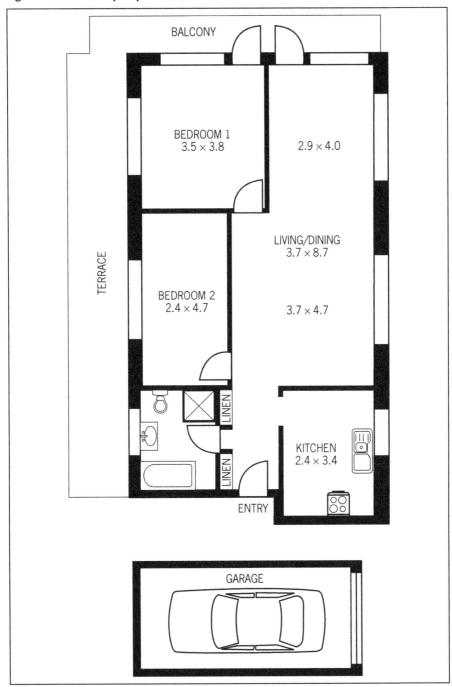

Source: Floor plan created by Bortex Pty Ltd

What you don't want to hear from your agent, especially when you are on holidays oceans away is, 'First, no-one is dead...there was a fire...the tenant left the towel over the heater and it caught on fire. There is damage to the room and smoke damage. All contained. However, the fire brigade did turn their hoses on a bit earlier than needed and a lot of carpet needs replacing'. The upshot: no-one was hurt and the insurance covered everything and we once again were glad we wrote that smoke alarms were to have batteries replaced on the agent's checklist of annual 'things to do'.

Growth without capital growth

This property was purchased in 2006 for $625 000 from another uninterested vendor. From our research we could see that the property had been bought in 2004 for $660 000 and the median in the area was $680 000. The property had been on the market for a long time. It looked like the worst house in the street. We assumed that the owner would not want to 'lose' money and would not sell for less than what they had bought it for — a psychological barrier. However, it turned out that they would. You can see the front — before and after — in figure 21.7. Notice how the 'new' window now fits the construction era.

In summary

The property was purchased for $625 000. The renovation was $116 000. This is obviously much higher than the usual '10 per cent' rule of thumb, however the high-end kitchen has become a feature of the property. The property was revalued 18 months later at $860 000, so technically the 15 per cent return on the renovation was evident based on the purchase price. However, the market dropped off and there was little capital gain in the period so all the added value came from the renovation and buying below the market. The capital growth since has added to this value. The original rent was $450 per week and, based on the renovation, the new rent was $820 per week. This property is positively geared even though all the funds were borrowed to complete the purchase and renovation. Who says you can't have a positively geared property with capital growth in a capital city? You can if you adopt the Trident Strategy.

Figure 21.7: our Kingsford house before (top) and after (bottom) renovation

This is something I have seen happen with my own property portfolio, but not something I have ever heard mentioned at a course or in a book: when a property starts nudging the high value mark (that is, $800 000), where it is a bit of a stretch for even middle Australians to afford, the rental return—which you would expect to be 4.5 to 5 per cent in capital cities—drops to about 3 per cent. Thus, when looking at your long-term property portfolio and cash-flow requirements note this when you do your calculations as it will have a major impact on your future cash flow and achieving your goals in your specified time frame.

Renovation rewards

As you can see, it is possible to have positively geared properties in growth areas. Although historically outer suburbs in capital cities have actually shown better growth, you need to do your numbers. Would you like 15 per cent per annum of $250 000 — that is, $37 500 per annum — or 7.5 per cent per annum of $800 000 — that is, $60 000 per annum? You need to work out your strategy and how it will get you to your goals. Maybe a few more affordable properties, spread across different areas with good growth projections are a good option (rather than one expensive property in one area). It all comes down to what suits your goals and your time frame for achieving them.

It's your turn

The fundamentals of property investing, at least as far as total return potential is concerned, apply to all property investments irrespective of whether an investor is buying for yield, buying for capital growth or renovating for profit. The most likelihood of realising strong total returns is with well-positioned properties yielding good rental returns, appealing to the owner-occupier and investor alike, that are reasonably close to amenities and urban centres. This is something I have emphasised in the book. Even regional investment opportunities can meet the latter criteria.

As with all investing, homework is critical to successful outcomes. Don't believe everything you hear or what you read; rather, check it out for yourself. Investing is about knowledge gathering. There are no easy answers. Locating a growth suburb requires a lot of time and research.

Visit <www.yourpropertysuccessnow.com.au/ypsbookbonus> to see more before and after photos and descriptions of completed renovations.

CHAPTER 22

Bringing it all together

Numbers lie at the heart of successful property investing. Regardless of whether your investment strategy is renovating for profit, building equity or another strategy, you have to crunch the numbers. The majority of investors who fail, do so because they guesstimate without fully understanding the implications of their financial position, or they depend on the hope strategy: buy, and hope it all works out.

It's at these times that we wonder what all this hard work is for. It is to compensate us for the effort we put in and to create some wealth for ourselves. But it should not be simply paper wealth just sitting there accumulating. You should aim to be in a position of not worrying about interest rates (despite all the noise in the media about interest rates), property prices, inflation or your day job. All of this should be about creating a mindset that is free of worry: that of genuine financial freedom (with *freedom* being the operative word).

There are as many views of the property market as there are property owners and quite frankly there is a lot of rubbish out there. But who do you trust? Trust yourself and your research. It all comes down to the numbers.

Some authoritative sources such as BIS Shrapnel suggest that residential real estate will grow quite strongly after the slowdown of the early 2010s, due to supply-and-demand factors. No doubt, affordability is again playing its part in growth. But no matter what the market is doing, there are always gems to be found. That's why in this book we focus on fundamentals: the need to find the locations that can, under examination, be expected to grow just before they become gems to make the most out of an investment at any time in the market cycle.

Many people start their property investing journey with cash-flow negative properties. And a typical property may cost a typical investor — let's say — $5000 per year. Typically, the cash flows do get better over time because while the depreciation benefits taper off, depending on which way you choose to calculate them, the rental income increases over time. And in recent years, good property in good areas has been subject to substantial increases in rental income. And that's likely to continue to be the case for the foreseeable future as demand outpaces supply for rental accommodation in many parts of Australia. The Trident Strategy will get you a positively geared property sooner.

The property cycle

Real estate is a long-term proposition for most investors. For sure there are opportunities for renovating for a profit, but for most investors the traditional route to wealth building in property is to buy well (the right property at the right price for you) and to hold for long-term capital appreciation.

A buy and hold strategy demands not only monitoring markets as a long-term holder but also extensive research before buying and analysing all the factors that you have researched to make sure you are in a position to hold for a period of time. Buy and hold strategies can be particularly powerful when properties are held through a full property cycle. Often, values can double or more through a cycle, validating the buy and hold approach.

Cycles, while not predictable to the point of exact timing, duration and magnitude, are extremely useful in anchoring our attitudes and views about real estate. Reading newspaper headlines can be a sucker-trap. They can seduce buyers into buying at the tops of markets when everybody is excited and at other times they can frighten would-be investors as media headlines forecast gloom and despair, publishing only bad-news stories.

It is crucial to know where you are in the property cycle. The property cycle, like other asset cycles (commodities, shares, and so on) tends to move in five- to-10-year intervals. In a cycle, property values can go from 'boom' to 'bust', but here is a closely guarded secret of successful property investors: they don't just buy in their back yard; they buy all over Australia. So when one market is booming, they are buying in another market that is bust.

At the early stage of a cycle (up part) prices usually rise before peaking. This is often the shortest phase of the cycle (often only a few years). Here, prices can increase rapidly (even up to 15 to 20 per cent per annum) but usually only for a year or two. Once they recognise this, investors see increasing property returns and compete with home buyers in the market. In the most recent boom we saw hundreds of thousands of first-time investors come into the market driven by generous government grants, property seminars, the press, television shows, and the like. The GFC arose from irresponsible lending practices in the US which created a bubble with over-optimistic buyers and less-than-professional financing strategies fuelling speculation.

It is important to understand that the property cycle does turn. Then, in bust conditions, astute and well-educated investors can find more opportunities to buy property at discounted prices. One indicator of where we are in a cycle is auction clearance rates (as well as days on market) which tend to decline after the boom period has subsided. It is a time when negotiating with vendors or their agents can be more profitable.

The key here is to understand that there is no place for emotion in property investing. Investors need to be aware that when headlines are screaming 'boom' and auction clearance rates are reaching 80 per cent or more, it is time to be more introspective. On the other hand, when 'doom and gloom' dominate the headlines and the feeling is one of despondency, it is time to sharpen the pencil and be alert to opportunities.

Developers are attuned to these shifting moods and cycles and they can be another useful indicator of where we are in the property cycle. When you start to see advertisements for 'free' trips to exotic locations where off-the-plan apartments can be bought for a 'bargain', take care: informed investors will always look to fundamentals and not to hype.

Revisiting the economic clock

Let's revisit the economic clock, which we learned about in chapter 4. See figure 4.3 on page 30.

The economic clock demonstrates that as an economy moves through the cycle, there is a time to buy certain types of investments and possibly a time not to buy.

For sure, turbulence can and probably will be encountered; this should be clear from what you have just read. Monitoring trends will not only enable you to view the value of your property in a broader context, but will allow you to monitor the market as whole, scanning for opportunities.

Monitoring your property and your cash

The most important thing in property investing—especially when you are building more assets (and more debt)—is that you think ahead.

$ Do not wait until you have run out of money and be forced to sell a property.

$ If a property is going to cost you huge dollars to repair and maintain (and will not be offset by capital growth) sell it *before* it becomes a problem.

$ Do not wait until interest rates have gone up so high you can't afford to hold the property—take some affirmative action.

$ Stay in touch with local councils (check their websites) so that you know what is happening with your area.

$ Revalue properties and refinance properties regularly and *before* adverse changes start to happen.

$ Do not over extend yourself. It's better to hold and manage a couple of properties than to have five and be forced to sell all of them!

$ Remember that property is a vehicle for getting you to your goals: it is not the goal. People who talk about their 10, 20 or more properties are most likely holding a portfolio of cheaper properties requiring a lot of unnecessary time and energy to manage. Don't get caught up in the 'how many do you have?' game.

Thinking ahead is the core to monitoring investments. How many times have you heard of stockmarket investors panicking and selling at the bottom of the market because they got spooked by one announcement? Many were likely overgeared or not monitoring their portfolio or the market. Take a big-picture approach to your investment property.

Putting on the work boots

The fact is, according to Australian Bureau of Statistics, fewer than 27 per cent of all property investors own more than one property, so you are setting a course that is outside of the norm. Although real estate investing can be a money-making prospect, for most people it is merely a dream. Well, in my view, dreams are for … dreamers!

Be a doer, not a dreamer. Put on your working boots. I believe in smart work, not hard work. Importantly I believe in consistent and informed investing and not in selling the dream of quick profits. Remember negative gearing remains one of the great enigmas of the investment market. It has been challenged from all fronts yet remains one of the bastions for high income earners to gain advantage of their top marginal rates in order to squeeze out returns and generate wealth.

The taxation system in Australia has a bias towards people gearing up: capital gains taxation concessions combined with negative gearing and depreciation allowances no doubt bias individual investors towards property. Indeed many high income earners are driven by their need to minimise tax rather than base their buying decision on sound investment principles.

Only a small percentage of the *BRW Magazine* Top 100 are people who made their first millions in property—but all those millionaires hold their millions in property. If it is good enough for them ...

The only really decent taxation deductions left in Australia are in investment property and superannuation.

The time and money conundrum

When I think about how little time there seems to be in our busy lives I wonder what the real gift of property wealth is. At the start of your property portfolio you set your goals. These are usually a dollar figure; that is, 'I want a passive income of $50000 per annum'. As you grow your portfolio you find that time becomes your new currency. For instance, 'Is it worth my while spending four weeks renovating when I can get a professional in who will do it in one week with a higher quality finish? And I'll get it rented faster, and be earning income and deducting the interest charges from that income sooner'. You will start appreciating where your efforts are best served and what is important to you.

Money gives you opportunities and choice. However, it can also give you time.

I think fondly of the time Todd surprised me with my fortieth birthday present. He realised a watch or a holiday or a 'thing' was not what I wanted or needed. In fact, I did not know what I wanted. He gave me the most amazing gift: 10 guilt-free days to be spend any way I wanted—time just for me, while he looked after our three-year-old son. He threw in some hints: go and visit my best friend in the US or go and attend one of those summer schools at Oxford on some obscure philosophy or archaeology subject (he also threw in a cheque for the plane trip). His gift to me was time and that was the best gift ever.

The truth is that 'poor' wage people prefer the security of a job with a steady salary or wage. They look for 'security' in knowing that there is a pay packet each and every week or month. But what is true is that this security comes at a price, and the cost is wealth and the freedom it brings to allow you to live the life that you deserve.

Mindset: it's your perspective that counts

Wealthy people prefer to get paid based on the outcomes of their investments or strategies and businesses; maybe not totally, but at least in part. The wealthy make income from their profits and this income is not wholly dependent on the number of hours they put in. Wealthy people pursue business opportunities in lieu of high salaries. Notice that there are no guarantees with any of the above; there is risk involved. You know that it's how you minimise that risk that will be your key to success. In fact, you have been given a tried and tested risk-minimisation strategy: the Trident Strategy.

Try this exercise: calculate your hourly work rate (your weekly income divided by the actual hours you work each week) — and be honest. Do you have that figure? Now do a calculation on a median property (for example, $433 000 with 5 per cent growth per annum) and how much you'd actually earn per hour if, for example, you put in 20 hours of management in the first year. At 5 per cent per annum growth it is $21 650 for 20 hours work, which is $1083 per hour. Nice work if you can get it. How does it compare with your hourly income?

Look at it another way. In the investment and business world, there is a cost for *not* taking a certain action. This is referred to as an opportunity cost. In other words, don't only evaluate the potential downside of action. It's equally important to measure the cost of inaction. If you don't pursue those things that excite you, where will you be in one year, five years, and 10 years? If you looked forward 10 years and know with 100 per cent certainty that it is full of disappointment and regret, then inaction is the greatest risk of all.

Expanding your thinking

A definition of wealth is to have the freedom of choice to do what you want, when you want: maybe you want to keep working, go on an endless holiday, start a new business. How do you define wealth? How do you want to spend your time? To me, time is the currency of wealth. Consider the currency that you are currently working with. Are you one of those people who spend all day looking for the cheapest product just to save a few dollars, or do you do a quick comparison of a product and its cost in a few places and make a decision, then move on? One person's currency is money; the other person's currency is time. As you move closer to achieving your goals, I can almost guarantee you will start working in the 'time is my currency' mindset.

People struggle financially because they act as if wealth is something outside of themselves over which they have no power. This is wholly a mindset issue. The main reason most Australians don't achieve financial independence is because 95 per cent of Australians just don't have the appropriate mindset.

Wealthy people create passive income streams by actualising their goals. This is built on a clear mindset of achievement—of action. They have streams of residual income—passive income—coming into their lives. One way to achieve this residual income is to buy well-located investment properties that are going to increase in value over the years.

In my property buying education business I am committed to encouraging big-picture thinking, but with an eye for detail. Incongruous? No way. I encourage the detailed research and investigation. For sure I have an eye for cash flow but I don't focus only on the net cash flow from investments. I look long term to the capital growth as well. The increasing equity of your property investments is as good as—if not better than—cash flow. We have learned that you can borrow against this increase in equity and use the funds just the same way you would use money earned in other ways—for example, as a deposit for further investments or even to live off.

Many beginning investors who don't understand this reality try to buy positive cash-flow properties rather than create them. By creating them using the Trident Strategy for low-risk property investing you quickly get to a positively geared property portfolio with capital growth thrown in.

There is no certainty in capital growth but the best indicator of future capital growth of any property in a particular area is the area's long-term track record of capital growth and a continuing growth in demand for rental properties as well as property sales.

Another common characteristic that wealthy, successful people have is that they recognise they can't do it alone. They know how to mobilise resources. They put people—a team—in place around them. And this can be extended even to social groups. Of course friends are friends, but time spent attending courses, going to networking groups and generally hanging around people who are positive and who look for ways of making things happen rather than reasons why things couldn't happen and people who can help push you beyond your comfort zone, is time well spent. Don't you wish more people would say, 'That is a great idea. When are you going to start? Why don't you call so-and-so and she can help you mobilise some more resources?'

Most really successful investors have mentors. Mentors (or coaches) create awareness in your mindset about things you can't see. Mentors help you break through barriers to realise your potential. Successful property investors have a team of people around them to help and to guide them and to help break through barriers to find their potential.

If you want to become a wealth creator, you are going to have to learn to think differently from the majority of people. You are going to have to learn to move outside your comfort zone. In fact, hopefully you have been challenged by some of the things in this book. On the other hand, you may just think, 'Ho hum. I've have seen it all before'. Regardless, you have come this far so you must be interested in the journey ahead.

Conclusion

Now your challenge is to keep it up. You may not be buying another property soon, or ever, but you are now embedded within the strategies and know-how to do so. It is your choice. Take your new skills and apply them in your life. Simply knowing the process of assessing risk—as we learned in the first chapters—and how to minimise consequences and evaluate likelihood can be applied to all that you do, even your career. In no time you will be coaching and encouraging your friends, maybe even meeting new friends who are also interested in creating a better future for themselves and their families, as you are.

This is your time. The time is yours to choose the life you want and to go and grab it with both hands. There is no better gift I can give you or you can give yourself, and your family and friends. I have been able to assist many of my close friends and family in following low-risk property investing strategies. They now have portfolios of varying sizes and they are growing their net wealth and getting closer to the lifestyles they want, sooner. This is what I wish for you. If anything, I hope that you take the teachings in this book and implement them, and that they help you achieve *Your Property Success with Renovation*.

Glossary

agent letting fees   These fees are charged by real estate agents for arranging the letting (rental) of a property.

agent management fees   These fees are charged by real estate agents for managing the ongoing rental of a property.

appraisal   A qualified person's opinion of the saleability of a property without them resorting to a full scale valuation.

appreciation   The increase in value of assets.

body corporate or owners corporation   The legal entity that manages a property that is part of a scheme (for instance, a strata, community or company title).

building inspector   A qualified person who inspects and reports on the quality of buildings on behalf of people seeking to purchase property.

buyer's agent   A licensed real estate agent employed specifically by the buyer to facilitate their property purchase.

capital gain   An increase in the value of an asset (for example, when the value of a house increases over time).

capital gains tax   Tax charged by the Australian Taxation Office on the increased value of investment assets (such as investment property).

caveat   This warns people, such as prospective buyers, mortgagees, and so on, who propose to deal in the land that a third person has a right or interest in the land.

compounding   The earning of interest on interest.

contract date   The date that the contract is exchanged and can be enforced.

cooling-off period   A period of time after the contract date that the purchaser can rescind the contract without incurring a major penalty, although a small penalty may still apply.

conveyancing   The act of transferring, assigning or engaging in dealings with respect to an interest in land.

council rates   Fees charged by local councils to land owners for services provided to local households (for example, garbage collection services).

cross-collaterisation   Often lenders will use multiple securities (for instance, your home and your investment property) to secure a new loan. This may save on lender's mortgage insurance but is often unnecessary and can restrict further portfolio growth for those with multiple purchases in mind.

default   This is the failure to meet an obligation when it is due. For example, a mortgage-holder is in default when they fail to make the required payment on their mortgage when it is due.

depreciation   The decrease in value of assets.

easement   The right a person has to use land belonging to another in a particular manner or a right to prevent the owner from using that land in a particular way.

equity   The difference between a property value and the loan. Available equity is the amount of equity an owner can actual access. This is usually based on the owner retaining 20 per cent equity in the property. This means they can only use 80 per cent of total equity, or more if they choose to use lender's mortgage insurance.

gearing   This is the use of borrowed money to fund investment. The more money you borrow, the more highly geared you are.

guarantor   A person who promises to pay the lender in case the borrower defaults.

inflation   The rise in prices of goods and services as measured by the Consumer Price Index (CPI).

insurance   Protection against the possibility of something going wrong, for example, fire destroying a property.

interest   The cost of borrowing money.

investment   Where you pay money (either yours or borrowed) into some form of money-making enterprise.

investment property   A commercial, residential, industrial or retail property that is primarily used for capital gain.

land tax   A tax payable on the value of land each year. This differs state by state and if the property is in an individual's name there is usually a threshold of land value before payable. In general, this is not payable on a principal place of residence.

lease   This is where you make regular payments for the right to use a particular item such as a car, house, and so on.

lender's mortgage insurance (LMI)   This type of insurance covers the lender in case a mortgage-holder defaults. Lenders charge this fee to clients; however they usually allow this one-off fee to be put on top of the loan (in other words, capitalising the LMI).

leverage   Using borrowed money to fund the purchase of an item (such as a house).

line of credit   A type of loan that essentially acts as a big credit card, that is, the mortgagor only pays interest on the outstanding balance not the entire limit. Often used to release available equity in a property.

loan to value ratio (LVR)   This is the loan secured by a property divided by the value of the property. Most lenders require an 80 per cent LVR for them to feel secure in their exposure. If the LVR is higher they take out lender's mortgage insurance or even self-insure.

negative gearing   This term is usually associated with property investing where total expenses exceed total income (resulting in a loss).

net worth   The net value of total assets minus total liabilities.

personal loan   Money borrowed from a financial institution (such as a bank) for a specific purpose such as the purchase of a car. The interest rate charged on a personal loan is usually higher than that charged on a mortgage because there is higher risk to the financial institution.

positive cash flow   This occurs when the cash coming in from an investment exceeds the cash going out.

principal and interest loan Repayment of a loan (generally associated with property investing) where both the interest and the amount borrowed are repaid together.

principal place of residence (PPOR) The property that you live in as your home, not an investment property.

private treaty sales A sale through negotiation via an agent as opposed to a sale by auction.

property management This is a division of a real estate office composed of leasing of space, collection of rents, selection of tenants and generally the overall maintaining and managing of real estate properties for clients.

property portfolio The total of all property investments by an individual (for example, a group or portfolio of properties).

quantity surveyor A person who undertakes the preparation of a statement of the quantities of material involved in the carrying out of construction work. A quantity surveyor also prepares tax depreciation schedules for investment properties.

return This is the reward you receive for investing in a certain product (for example, interest received on an interest bearing deposit).

risk A calculation based on the likelihood and consequences of an action. This involves the probability that something will not go according to plan.

risk tolerance The level of risk an individual is willing to take. Generally the higher the return, the higher the risk.

settlement The transfer of title (ownership) of property.

sinking fund These are funds allocated by the body corporate of a strata building to pay for maintenance or an upgrade of the building.

stamp duty A state based government tax charged on various things such as the purchase of a property (usually when there is a change of ownership).

standard variable rate of interest This is the undiscounted rate of interest charged by a financial institution when it lends money.

strata title This is a form of ownership devised for multi-level apartment blocks and horizontal sub-divisions with shared areas, or lots. These lots can be applied to unit blocks, high-rise apartments, townhouses, duplexes, factories, retail shops, and so on.

subdivision   An area of real estate divided into lots.

tenant   A person who leases a property and pays a regular fee called rent.

valuer   A qualified person responsible for establishing the value of specific properties. Financial institutions usually have a panel of valuers that they use to value properties for the purpose of lending.

valuation   A valuation is the result of a valuer establishing the value of a property. The valuer prepares a report clearly identifying the estimated value of a property. Only registered, valuers can provide valuations.

variable loan   This is a loan that has an interest rate that moves with changes to the Reserve Bank of Australia's cash rate, or even at the discretion of a lender.

vendor   The seller of an asset such as a property.

yield   The profit or income (usually annual) that an investment property provides. The yield is normally expressed as a percentage of the property value.

zoning   Various geographical areas are 'zoned' by local councils. This is simply a way of establishing what land can be used for. For example, zoning may be 'residential' which means only property designed for living in can be built in that area.

Index

assets 22–23 *see also* liabilities
— good debt versus bad debt 23
— net 17
Association of Superannuation
Funds of Australia, The 17
Australian Property Investor 93, 96
Australian Property Monitors
132, 135
average family statistics 6

BIS Shrapnel 4, 213
body corporate 38, 140, 144–145, 199
borrowing capacity 24, 65–69
see also lenders
— affordability and gearing 70–71
— calculator 71
— determining 69–73
— lenders' mortgage insurance
(LMI) 72–73
— living costs 69–70
— rental income 69
— savings history 72
budgeting 19–22, 23
— discretionary spending 20, 21
— tips 23–25
building inspections 131, 138–141,
197–198 *see also* pest inspections;
purchasing your property
buy and hold strategy 6, 33–34,
118, 214

buyer's agent 86, 133
buying criteria 55–61
— capital growth 185
— demographics 56–57
— for units 60–61
— market 59
— personal 60
— property investing 57–59
— specifics 57–60
buy, renovate and hold strategy
122–124 *see also* renovation
strategies
— versus flipping strategy
124–125
buying your property *see* purchasing
your property

capital gains tax 11, 17, 35, 36, 217
— and renovation strategies
117–124
capital growth 7–8, 9, 219 *see also*
rule of 72; Trident Strategy
— and buying criteria 56, 58–59
— and cash flow 8–9
— and locating a property
88–89, 91, 96
— and renovation 117, 163, 181
— versus yield 36–38
cash-flow management *see*
budgeting

cash-flow tracker 23, 24
contract of sale 131, 133, 136,
    143, 166
  —'subject to finance'
    clause 136
conveyancing 143
cooling-off period 122, 138
costs of purchase, example 75
credit file 70, 71, 121, 137
Cupit, Leon 138–139

demographics 56–57, 101–108
  —example 105
  —what to look for 103–104
deposit 20, 68, 137 *see also* lenders;
    lenders' mortgage insurance
  —loan approval 75–76
  —risk 46, 53

economic clock 30–31, 215
  —example 77
equity *see also* Trident Strategy
  —building your portfolio
    124
  —in other properties 66, 67,
    68, 76, 123
  —and lender's mortgage
    insurance 84
  —model 76–78
  —renovation 52, 81, 98, 99,
    151–152, 195
  —renovation strategies 117,
    121, 122, 124–125
  —rental yield 59–60
  —and types of loans
    78–79, 80
  —valuation 191–192
exit strategy 5, 11–12, 15–17, 49, 51
    see also goals; income, passive;
    Trident Strategy

finances 19–25 *see also* budgeting
  —cash buffer 24
  —cash flow 23
  —credit cards 24
  —increasing your income 24–25
  —spending 23, 24
finishes 126–127 *see also*
    renovation potential
flipping strategy 34, 35, 106,
    117–122 *see also* buy, renovate
    and hold strategy; renovation
    strategies
  —example 118
  —financing 121
  —hidden costs 119–121
  —versus buy, renovate and hold
    strategy 124–125
future rental income,
    estimating 59

goals 3 *see also* budgeting
  —defining 13–15
  —establishing your 11–17
  —income 6, 11
  —setting 12–13

heritage overlay 115, 188, 200
high-rise unit developments 39
'honeymoon' loan *see* loans,
    types of
house versus unit 38–39 *see also*
    property investment strategies

income, passive 7, 9, 11, 17,
    35, 40
Independent Property
    Inspections 138
inspecting properties 109–113
  —inspection checklist 109–110,
    111, 129

landlord's insurance 51, 146
legal advice 136, 143
lenders 66–67, 136
—borrowing capacity
    calculator 71
—example 72
—exposure 85–86
—pre-approval 137
lender's mortgage insurance 72–73,
    79, 84
letter of offer 131, 136, 140–141
    see also contract of sale
liabilities 22–23
loan approval 75–86
—equity model 76–78
—example costs 75
—professional help 86
—property finance 78
—types of loans 78–84
loan-to-value ratio (LVR) 68
loans, types of 78–84
—comparison rates 82
—fixed rate 83–84
—interest rates 81–82
—offset accounts 82–83
—principal and interest versus
    interest only 80
local council 39
location 49–50 see also
    demographics; property
    performance factors
—capital growth 96–97
—hot spots 90–92
—identifying suburbs 106–108
—population growth 95
—rental demand 95–96
—supply 96

mindset 14–15, 218 see also goals
monitoring your property 216

off the plan 34, 39

pest inspections 138–141 see also
    building inspections; purchasing
    your property
property as an asset 4
property cycle 214–215
property finance, understanding 78
property insurance 146
property investment strategies
    6, 33–41
—buy and hold 33–34
—defining 36–41
—flipping 35
—renovation 35
—risk–reward graph 36
—selecting 34–35
property managers 172–173
property performance factors
—capital growth 88–89
—rental yield 89
—scarcity 89
property portfolio, building
    process 16
purchasing your property 131–141
—building and pest inspections
    138–141
—buying below the market 134
—making an offer 134–138
—the process 143–147
—what to ask the agent 132–133
—what to consider 131–132

quantity surveyor 165–166
quotes 178

renovating tips 165–175
—bathrooms 170
—first impressions 166
—fittings and fixtures 171–172

renovating tips (*cont'd*)
— floor plans 167
— kitchens 171
— painting 167–168
— quantity surveyor 165–166
— skylights 169
— 'wow' expenses 173–175
renovation, categories of 152–155
renovation, costing your 157–164
see also renovation, valuing your
— percentage profit and costs
159–164
— professional support
158–159
— profit 157–158
renovation, examples of 197–212
renovation, organising your
177–185
— budget 178
— delays 179, 180, 181
— getting started 177–178
— planning 179–182
— safety net 184–185
— scheduling 182–183
renovation potential 115–129
— assessing properties
125–129
— choosing properties 116
— rejuvenation strategy 129
— repair strategy 128–129
renovation, reviewing your
187–189
Renovator's Report 116
renovation strategies 35, 40–41,
116–124 *see also* buy, renovate
and hold strategy; flipping
strategy
— comparing 124–125
renovation, valuing your 172,
189–195

rental income 7, 8, 132
rental risk 46–48 *see also* risk;
Trident Strategy
rental yield 51–52, 89
research 4, 92–99
— property websites 134
Residex 116, 135
retirement myth, the 5
risk 27–32 *see also* Trident
Strategy
— assessing 28
— economic clock 30–31
— minimising 31
— tolerance 28–29
RP Data 135
rule of 72 7–8, 9

Salt, Bernard 105
serviceability 68 *see also* borrowing
capacity; lenders
settlement period 131
Smart Property Investment 93
strata title 144
— management fees 60
— report 144–145
strategies 3
'subject to finance' clause 136

tenants 133
tradespeople 178, 181
Trident Strategy 43–53, 117, 181,
201, 203
— and buying below market
value 43, 52, 93, 113, 134
— and capital growth 43, 52,
113, 210
— and renovation 43, 52, 98,
113, 115, 151–156, 184
— risk, minimising 48–53
— risk, types of 45–48, 218

units, buying criteria 60–61

vacant possession 136
valuer *see* renovation, valuing your
vendor 132 *see also* purchasing your
  property

yield versus capital growth 36–38
  see also property investment
  strategies
Your Investment Property 93

Homebuyers and Investors

Can you afford not to buy the right property at the right price?

Confused about how to go about getting into the home of your dreams or establishing a property portfolio that allows you to be financially free? Wondering what the next step is? Wondering how you can create your own plan and work through what you need to do to get to the next step?

Educating yourself on how to build your property portfolio should not be expensive. Your Property Success is all about making quality education affordable and achievable; with easy to follow courses and exercises so you end up with your own specific blueprint. These online courses make it absolutely possible for you to go from confusion to action in just 6 weeks.

The five essential courses can be purchased individually or as a package at a discount. Inside you'll get six bite-sized modules per course, where we'll show you how to:

- Define what you want and how to get there.
- Work out how each property purchase gets you to your goal.
- Create a property portfolio based on low-risk principles.
- Add value to your portfolio in the short, medium and long term.

You can get started any time from now and you can work at your own pace. You work through the manuals and workbooks when it suits you, in the comfort of your home. To make it even easier for you, all the courses are available online and also downloadable to Kindle and iPad.

We are so convinced of the quality and value, we're giving you access to some great training videos. Scan the code at right or visit www.yourpropertysuccessnow.com.au

Courses can be downloaded to Kindle or iPad

Check out the courses at www.yourpropertysuccess.com.au

Helping you invest
in your future

Founded by Australian property expert Jane Slack-Smith, Investors Choice Mortgages is an award-winning mortgage broking company owned and run by experienced finance professionals.

We are investors ourselves and we understand that each and every client's situation is unique. We take the time to understand your goals and your own personal circumstances so we can help you with the finance solution that not only fits your needs now, but also sets you up with the future in mind.

At Investors Choice, we believe that education is the key to a successful property purchase, so on top of our expert finance advice we also provide our clients with ongoing resources and tools to help them achieve the outcomes they desire.

We have helped thousands of Australians purchase their first home, their first investment property and in more than a few cases, their 2nd, 3rd or 4th investment property.

And we'd love to help you too.

"A great experience that took the stress out of loan selection and application. They analysed and then explained all our options in a professional yet simple to understand manner."

No question too simple or too silly

Call us to discuss your property purchase and find out why our clients keep on coming back

1800 46 48 10 | www.investorschoice.com.au

Investors Choice Mortgages